L I F E:

ITS PROBLEMS

&

Some of its Unanswerable Questions

To: Ellie & Don

Thank You Yes from Choices & Best Wishes for your future!

Dr. Mick M Rowy

LIFE:

ITS PROBLEMS

&

Some of its Unanswerable Questions

Dr. Nicholas La Bianca

Copyright © 2008 by Dr. Nicholas La Bianca.

ISBN:	Hardcover	978-1-4363-7229-9
	Softcover	978-1-4363-7228-2

All rights reserved. No part of this book may be reproduced or transmitted in any form or by any means, electronic or mechanical, including photocopying, recording, or by any information storage and retrieval system, without permission in writing from the copyright owner.

This book was printed in the United States of America.

To order additional copies of this book, contact:
Xlibris Corporation
1-888-795-4274
www.Xlibris.com
Orders@Xlibris.com
53565

Contents

Chapter I	Who Are We? Why We Are Here? Where Did We Come From?	1
Chapter II	Who Is God? How Did He Get There? Why Did He Create the World in which We Live? What Does He Expect Us to Do and Why?	7
Chapter III	The Universe	12
Chapter IV	Religion and Its Role in Our Lives	17
Chapter V	The Human Race	26
Chapter VI	The Individual Human Being	31
	Observations I	38
	Dance Like No One's Watching	40
Chapter VII	Nationality	41
Chapter VIII	Government	47
Chapter IX	Politics	55
Chapter X	Justice	63
Chapter XI	Education	69
Chapter XII	Possible Solutions	73
	a) Part I: On the Financial Aspect of the Problem	73
	b) Part II: On the Educational Aspect of the Problem	77
	c) Part III: Social and Civil Right Changes	81
Chapter XIII	Additional Questions on Customs, Traditions, and Morality	84
	Observations II	88
Chapter XIV	Improvements on the Social Services	90
Chapter XV	Dealing With Crime and Punishment	96
Chapter XVI	Reality Check	100

In loving memory of my son Angelo, my mother Maria,
my father Angelo, and my brother Peppino.
May they rest in peace!

PREFACE

During our early years, we accept without reservation all the explanation that our parents or religious leaders give us about our life on this earth. Later on we get involved with our future, and all our efforts are directed in making sure that we develop our talents and acquire all the skills necessary to have a very comfortable life. Our daily lives as adults are always under stress from the demands of our jobs, our families, and other related problems that we have to face. Most of our recreational time is spent on hobbies, vacations, and sports events; and very rarely, we try to find an answer for our existence in this world. The believers find all the answers in their religion, some of the non believers create their own ethical and moral rules of behavior, and others do not care to find any answers, and their only desire is to make their lives as comfortable as possible even at the expense of other human beings. This creates an unbalance in the relation among people with the relative, selfish, immoral, and unethical practices that make life difficult for all. Regardless, there is a time in our lives when we try to find answers to the reason why life exists on earth. Even for those people who accept the fact that we are here to serve the Lord, still there is a need to explain why there is a god, where did he come from, why there is a universe and how it was created, why he creates us, what is the purpose of our life, and how we should live it to fulfill our destiny.

While we are finding all sorts of rational explanations to the physical world around us for these questions, no one has come up with a universally acceptable one. It is only when we are facing death that we wonder about if there is life after death, and what is all about. Some accept it with serenity since their life has been according to the rules imposed by their religion, others try to repent at last moment in order to avoid some possible horrible punishment from the higher authority, and others don't care about anything and believe that at that point it is the end of everything.

The Birth of Venus

CHAPTER I

Who Are We? Why We Are Here? Where Did We Come From?

These and many other questions very often come to our minds, and each one of us tries to answer them in our own way. Going back to the beginning of civilization, we found that almost every generation has produced philosophers who believed to have found the answers to these and other questions; and thanks to their efforts, we have reached certain truths about the human race and the world around us. The first attempts to understand God took place among the civilizations of the Orient, but they failed in their intent because they combined myths with religion.

The Greeks were the first to establish schools of thought that tried to solve the problem in a rational way. Their attention was first directed at explaining the natural world and solving the problem of *arkhe*, which was supposed to be the beginning of everything. Thales of Miletus, one of the three Milesian natural philosophers from the Ionian School (sixth century BC), was the first to come up with the idea that "water" was the basic material from which all things originated, and he also stated that the soul (psyche) was the force (*kinetikon*) that moved things. He seemed to be quite advanced with other researches since, according to Herodotus, he predicted the solar eclipse of 585 BC. With Pythagoras and his school (550-500 BC), the search for a rational universal principle was also directed to politics, religion, sciences, and education. For them, the universe was under strict mathematical order; and being so, it created harmony and beauty. From then on, there was a succession of philosophers rejecting and changing the findings of their predecessors, and it would be too long a list to explain. It was only with the Sophists that ethics came into existence, particularly with Socrates.

The Parthenon

Anything that we know about him was passed on by Plato. Most interesting are the so-called Socratic paradoxes in which the philosopher declares that virtue is wisdom or knowledge, and that no one does anything wrong willingly, and bad actions are only caused by lack of knowledge. Evidently, his philosophical views and his association with some of the aristocratic party in Athens were not very well accepted by his countrymen. He was brought to trial on charges of introducing strange gods and corrupting the youth, and was condemned to death. He was given a chance to escape during the thirty days between his trial and execution, but he refused to break the laws of Athens; and believing that he had done nothing wrong with his teachings, he drank the poison and died with a smile on his face (399 BC).

LIFE: ITS PROBLEMS & SOME OF ITS UNANSWERABLE QUESTIONS

Socrates

It was only with Plato (429-347 BC) and his school, the Academy, and later with Aristotle (384-322 BC.) with his Lyceum, that the basis of modern philosophy with moral, metaphysical, ethical, and political issues were laid out,; and from that time on, they have been the main spheres of interest of medieval, renaissance, and modern Western philosophy. For centuries, thousands and thousands of philosophers, theological scholars, writers, astronomers, and others who have been discussing, changing, adding, creating different theories; and some of them believed to have found answers to many of these questions. But except for the scientific field where we have made some incredible progress, the rest of the explanations do not give us any definite and rational answers. Since mankind has not been able to find a scientific and rational answer to explain his presence in this world, many individuals have found answers in their religious beliefs, and there are no problems for them. It is a blessing that most of the world population belongs to some religious entities that preach some fair and acceptable rules of behavior, and life goes on in spite of so many conflicts. However, while some religions try to convert the nonbelievers with a loving and rational way, others may be driven by the fact that they have a mission: to convert the nonbelievers by any possible means, including violence. This creates an impossible situation since God created man with a "free will," and it is not acceptable that one person should impose his beliefs on another. All-important religions base their roots on the "direct" instructions from God, which were transmitted to them through scriptures and other revelations. When this "truth" is accepted, then there is no way to question the Word of God, and it is the believer's duty to live by it and to spread the truth to the rest of the world in any way possible.

Blessed are those who have faith in their religion since their lives are simple, overflowing with love; and no hardship can upset their lifestyles because they know what is right and what is wrong, and how to behave under all kinds of circumstances. Due to their hard work and impeccable behavior, the whole world goes on toward the right direction achieving progress and better life conditions for all human beings. Still, there are differences among all existing religions since each one claims to be the only true way to serve God. For centuries, religious leaders have been rationalizing, creating, and finding evidence that what they preach is the only truth since they received their instructions directly from God. At this point, it seems the problem reaches an impasse since all religious leaders' claims that their own particular worship is the only way to serve God; and unless God itself somehow points out the true answers, the conflict will go on forever. From a practical point of view, it is clear that not everybody has the chance to choose his own religion. The choice is almost all the time an accident of birth. The newborn is always raised according to the religion of his parents, and the intensity of the training received while growing up will always determine the strength of his faith for the rest of his life. Of course, many change their religion at some point during their lifetime, but this is an exception rather than the rule.

As everything else in this world, nothing is perfect; so among the religious people, we find a large range of followers that goes from the fanatics to those who merely belong to a religion because of tradition or some other insignificant reason. If a person does not have a strong faith, he may challenge the claim that any religion has a direct link to God, or may challenge many popular explanations that we hear about the beginning and the evolution of the world. For example, it is said that he created the world in six days and rested on the seventh. Did he really get tired of working for six days? If so, there is a limit then to his power, and then he is not the same God as we know him. He created man from dust and the

LIFE: ITS PROBLEMS & SOME OF ITS UNANSWERABLE QUESTIONS

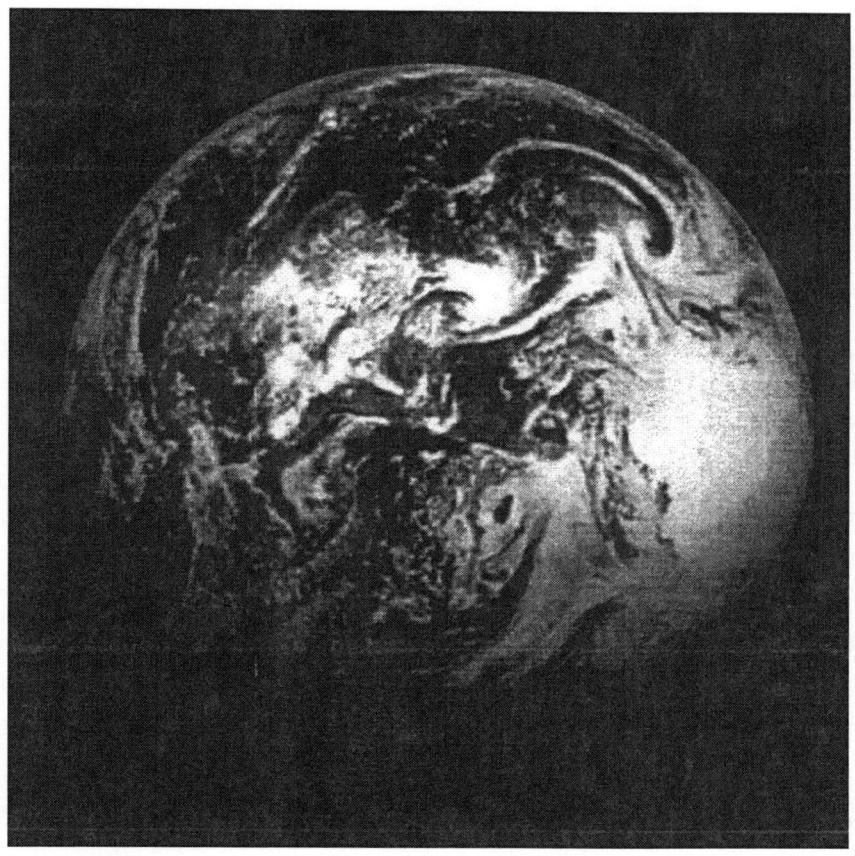

The earth

woman from his rib. Did he really need the dust and the rib to do so? Was there anyone observing his actions, and if not, how do we know it? He created man in his image. Do we really look like God? Has anyone seen God? It is said that Adam and Eve had two sons. How these two sons populated the world? How about the promise of God not to destroy any city with more than three honest persons in it while the entire nations and populations were annihilated during the past centuries? How about Noah's ark that some people are still trying to locate? It must have been tremendously big to contain two animals of each species and all the food necessary to keep them alive for forty-five days. And all these were accomplished by Noah with just the help of his son. There are also questions that refer to the future. When the good Lord decides to end this world, there will be a "judgment day." We will take back our bodies and go in front of him who will decide how we will spend the rest of our eternal life. Since everybody dies at a different age—some very young, other in the middle age, and others very old—what age will we be reincarnated? If so, since most of the people die of old age, the whole group will be made up by an old—and ugly looking mob. Are we going to keep the same relationship with the members of our family? Are we going to keep the same sex, or are we going to be asexual? How are we going to be reorganized? What are we going to be doing with our time? And if we do not take back our bodies, then no corporal punishment can be administered, and the poor Dante Alighieri in his *Divina Commedia* wasted all that time, showing us how the sinners were going to be punished in the circles of his inferno. The truth is that nobody ever came back to tell about the "other life," and what we hear is strictly a product of excited fantasies. There are few people that claim to have died for a brief period of time, in one case it lasted one whole hour. One of them states that he went to heaven, another went to hell, and both describe the two different places. Frankly, their descriptions can be considered a good and a bad dream, respectively, and dismissed as such. These and many other questions may come up now and then, and it is very difficult to find a rational answer for them. At this point, some people accept everything presented by their religion as absolute truth since God is capable of doing anything, others give up any pretense of being religious, and others accept it with some reservation because as one person said about superstition, "I don't believe in it, but why take a chance, there is nothing to lose in following some of its rules."

CHAPTER II

Who Is God? How Did He Get There? Why Did He Create the World in which We Live? What Does He Expect Us to Do and Why?

The creation of Adam

If we had answers to these questions, then we would understand God; and in being able to do so, God would not be what he is. At the same time, we never stopped seeking answers to these questions. From the beginning of time, men have seen God in the surrounding nature and in everything else that they could not understand and explain. The sun, moon, rain, winds, earthquakes, volcanoes, oceans, etc., were considered supernatural entities, and men did their best to keep them happy with sacrifices and other ceremonies. Even now in some remote areas of the world where people live in a primitive state, we find natives worshipping the spirits of the forest, some of the animals living in it, mountains, etc. At some point, in the western part of the world surfaced more organized religions such as those of the Egyptians, the Greeks, and the Romans who worshiped several gods for many centuries. Then came the ones who were based on the Old Testament and recognized only one God. Looking at the history, it seems that the new God cared and protected just one nation, ignoring the rest of mankind that also had been created by him. At later dates, new prophets came around to show the world the proper way to worship God and how to live according to his rules.

Now we have the followers of each different religious faction claiming to have historical data to prove that they are the only followers of the true prophet, and we end up with different groups claiming "we are right and you are wrong," basing on a great amount of evidence that proves their religion to be the only true one. Since these different groups live mainly in different geographic areas, it is evident that if they were born in another area, they would believe in a different religion according to the one existing at their birthplace; hence, we have to accept the fact that, in general, religion is picked up by "accident" of birth. Someone born in East Asia for sure will have a different religion from one born in Middle East, or one born in Europe. And even within a geographical area, some religions split into different factions; and in almost all cases, the parents decide on the choice of worship. Before we reach maturity, we are indoctrinated into one "true" religion without having had any choice in the process. Many ignore all these issues and live their lives strictly according to their material needs, and others spend their lives trying to find some answers to the above-mentioned questions; and since all of us have different backgrounds, level of intelligence, and education, we can end up creating our own personal religion.

Fortunately, most of the largest existing religions believe in one God, and this may help us find a solution to this very critical problem. Having established this, for the sake of the argument, we can visualize people of different religions worshipping God in their own different ways, and the good Lord looking down at them. It is not fair to conclude that he would prefer one form of worship to another. As a matter of fact, no one can believe that God is very much entertained by our dancing, singing, sacrificing, and other forms of worship. It may satisfy us because as humans we would perceive them as a gesture of love and good will, but God wants something else, and we can only speculate about it. Many religions claim that they have the right answers, and that if people do not worship according to their rites, they will be condemned and will not be able to go to heaven. Since millions of people have lived in isolation and have never heard or have been exposed to others religions, it would not be fair to punish them for not knowing the "right" way to worship the Lord. We must conclude that if they are sincere and they live their lives in the proper way, God would accept their prayers regardless of the way they are offered to him. It seems that what is demanded by God is how we live and the purpose of our lives. So the whole problem rests in our own individual "self" and the standards we set for ourselves. Still, the main question is: how can we live the proper way and best serve the Lord? Well, in order to answer that question we have to ask ourselves what is the final destiny of the human race.

From a rational, historical, and scientific point of view, we really do not know why we are here, and for what reason. The only truth that we can come up with is that by looking at the history of the human race, we see that mankind has been trying to improve life in the world in which we live. We have come a long way. From the early days when food and staying alive were the main goals of each day, we have come to the point where food and safety are taken for granted, at least in the more developed countries of the world. There is much more work to do to bring the whole world to those standards. It has not been easy to reach this point, and we are still struggling to bring some sort of balance within the existing nations. The stronger and better advanced civilizations have always been able to overpower the weaker nations and use them to their own advantage; therefore, we have to conclude that knowledge is power and helps to make life more comfortable, and ignorance has a negative result on the struggle for a better life. The same scenario repeats in the individual daily life. Those people with knowledge and talents are always in control, always in the lead, and always live a better life while the ignorant are at their service. In view of the above, we have to conclude that the only destiny of man is to gain knowledge and thus gain control of the nature around us and learn to use it for our own benefit.

From a religious point of view, we could say that God wants us to become "good people" and live according to his rules. But what is the purpose of this objective? If he wanted us to be "good," he would have had no problem in making us "good" to begin with. Maybe he was bored and decided to play a game by creating the human race, give us some intelligence and an environment in which to live, and see how far we could go in improving ourselves. So what are the limits to our progress in our world? We can only rely on the nature around us, and our experience from the past. We have been able to decode the mechanism that brings changes in the natural world, but still we are unable to explain how it all came about to be, so we have to accept the fact that a supernatural being created it, and the whole thing is behind any human understanding. Looking back at our past, we have to admit that humans have come a long way in understanding the surrounding natural world and using this knowledge to improve our living conditions. The more we learn, the more control we have on nature, and we use it to improve our quality of life. Many of us take for granted our progress and not very often reflect on the progress made by the human race since the beginning of life on this planet. Even when civilization thought they had achieved the highest degree of lifestyle and discoveries, it becomes insignificant if we compare them with the present-day achievements. Imagine if someone had told a Roman that someday we would be able to see and talk to another person on the other side of the earth, thanks to the miracle of television. Even if someone with great imagination had come up with this vision, the response of the public at that time would be that only the gods would be able to achieve such feats. So for them at that time, we would have had the same power as the gods. Even if at this time our technical achievement seems to be incredibly outstanding, it will become insignificant compared to the one that we will be able to enjoy in the next few hundreds years.

In view of the enormous progress obtained so far, it would be conceivable that some day humans could be in complete control of the natural laws that exist in this planet. We can envision the day that we may be able to control the weather and all the other elements on this earth and create anything that our physical body needs. On the base of the new genetic discoveries, we can imagine a time in the future when we can create a perfect human being with any desired characteristics as far as his physical appearance is concerned. We may create human beings immune to any disease and that may live longer and longer and never become old and someday be able to live forever. And since the modern way of traveling makes it impossible to go to other planets behind our life span, maybe we will be able to move around using the power of our mind. For example, I could close my eyes and think of being anywhere in the world, and I can do this instantaneously. In the future, we may be able to find a way to do the same thing and move immediately anywhere we want to go, and this idea is not a product of the fantasy since scientists are studying the existence of new "dimensions" in the universe and the possibility of traveling into the past.

It seems that we have the potential of becoming immortal, and somehow we have in us a potential divine nature that will unite us to God, whatever he may be. We can compare human beings to the cells in a body. Each cell has a distinct function, and when it dies, a new cell is created to keep the body alive. Some cells have more important and vital functions than others, but each one is as important as the others for the well-being and the life of the body. The same can be said about the human race. Each individual is like a cell in the body. Some have more important roles than others, but one thing is sure, and that is all must be working toward the final goal of the human race, which, according to what has been presented before, is to be united and become part of God.

If we dismiss the above as a product of an excited imagination, then we can speculate that from a practical point of view, the purpose of our lives is to take charge of the natural world around us, to reach a point where we can eliminate any kind of uncomfortable situation from our lives, and to use to the fullest all the means that God gave us to reach the state of happiness, which at this time we are not able to clearly understand.

CHAPTER III

The Universe

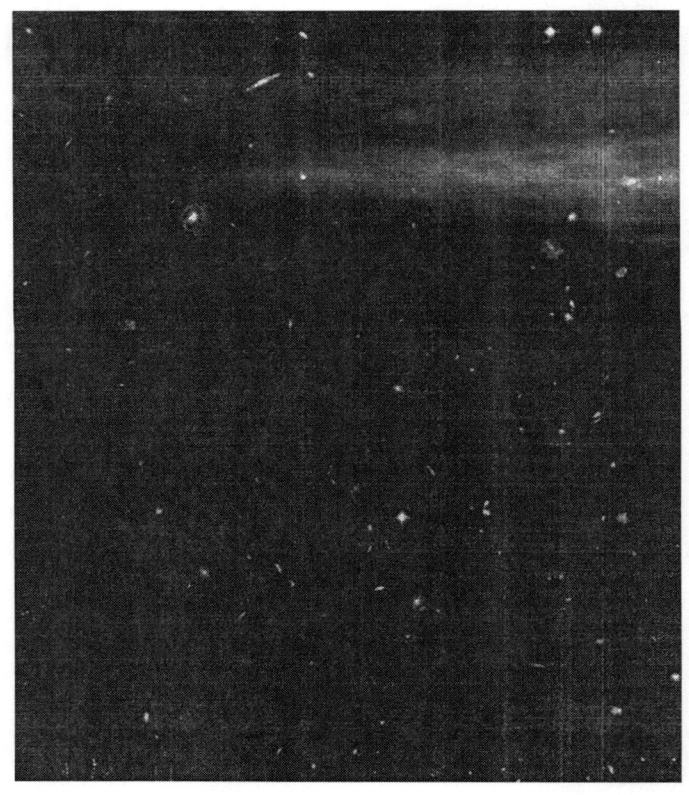

The universe

In order to fulfill our destiny, it is absolutely necessary that we understand the universe around us—how it came about to be, what it is made of, and how it functions. For centuries, we have been looking at the sky for answers, and we must agree that we have made great advances, but also we are very far for a rational explanation. We have been able to trace the origin of the universe through big bang when from the explosion of a single speck of dust, it became the expanding universe as we perceive it now. With our powerful telescopes, we have been able to identify an enormous amount of galaxies and stars. The latest information we have about our own galaxy, the Milky Way, shows that it contains two hundred billions of stars, and among these stars and planets are at least six billions similar to our solar system. In addition to our own, there are two hundred more identified galaxies spread out all over the universe, which are running away from its center at incredible speed. Thinking about their numbers and distances is something incomprehensible for us, especially when they say that there are more stars than

Galaxy

grains of sand on the earth and are billions of light-years away from one galaxy to another. We can also speculate that since among all those stars with other planets similar to ours, there may be other developed civilization living in them. We even have made several attempts to get in touch with them, and we are constantly beaming radio signals into space, hoping that someone out there may be able to receive them. And if their civilization is more advanced than ours, perhaps they could attempt to get in touch with us. Unfortunately, the distances are so great that at the speed of light, it would take several generations of people to reach the nearest star.

With all the knowledge acquired through the centuries, still no one has been able to tell us how the big bang came about. There must be a beginning to everything, and no one has been able to explain how and why it all began. Add to it that most of what we see in the sky happened billions of light-years ago, and it is now reaching us, it is very possible that it may have changed or perhaps is not there anymore. Facing these extreme situations that our mind is not able to absorb, many people decide to go back to religion and accept the fact that the good Lord created this world for us to enjoy, and for them that is the end of it. As a matter of fact, at this time, there is a big debate in the courts between two different factions. Some are demanding that the school should teach and explain the world in which we live only according to the theory of evolution, and others requesting that the theory of intelligent design should be included. What a waste of human resources! Why not present both points of view and let the students decide what to believe.

If we take a close look at these different points of view, we will see that both have valid arguments that could make them acceptable up to a certain point. In the theory of evolution, we can clearly see that scientists have come a long way in identifying and explaining the laws of nature. We know now how the mountains were formed and what causes the earthquakes. We can predict the weather based on all the information we have on the ocean currents and atmospheric conditions, and above all, we have decoded the law of gravity, which is the basic power that drives the whole universe and keeps everything running and under control. Apparently, we can trace animal life to its origin, from the most complex back to its basic simple cell and can explain all the changes based on the need to survive in the existing environment. Still, it does not completely satisfy the need for a rational explanation of the life around us. There are too many missing links from the original beings into the present ones.

On the other end, when we observe the beautiful nature and life in the world around us, we know that the whole thing did not come about from chaos but from some rational and great mind that created the whole thing according to an intelligent design. From the most complex molecule down to the barest atom, and further we can see how everything is controlled by certain laws that make everything happen and there must be some "force" behind it to make it all happen. Scientists can explain all the changes that occur practically in everything but still do not know how and why. Even people who do not believe in God have to admit that some "force" is behind the whole universe, and it is behind our capabilities to know how and why the whole thing came to be. In our daily life, we have become so accustomed to everything around us that we very rarely stop and think about them. Just pick up a tiny little flower and try to figure out how from a tiny little seed and some soil we'll have such a beautiful creation with infinity of shapes, colors, and fragrances that bring us such delightful sensations.

Nature

Anyone studying or reading about astronomy is mesmerized by the continuous use of millions and billions of light-years, stars, galaxies, and other celestial bodies. The continuous changes, collisions, and explosions that occur and the release of those unconceivable amount of energy are behind human comprehension. Even when they talk about the solar system, the time it took to become so, and the time left until it comes to an end, is expressed in millions of years. At first, it gives us a very comfortable feeling of security because our life span is insignificant compared to those numbers, but then we come across the unpredictable possibilities of natural accidents or changes that can annihilate the whole earth in matter of seconds. The most probable one is the fall of a large meteorite on the earth that, as in the past, can create unlivable conditions and destroy all living organisms. Even if we can predict it, if its size is big enough, there is no way we can do anything about it. And then there are the possibilities of the sun getting too close to earth and vaporizing everything, or the moon getting away from us, and the earth cooling off and not being able to retain the force of gravity that keeps everything in its proper place.

During the last few years, a new threat to mankind has appeared: global warming. Some say that the warming is a natural phenomenon, and others say that it is man made. All nations seem to be concerned, and the United Nations is actively involved trying to find a solution to the problem. Every year several meetings are scheduled all over the world. There are lots of suggestions, several recommendations, many promises, but very few nations are willing to do something about it because it requires a great amount of financial resources. Meanwhile, the glaciers are slowly but steadily melting, and the level of the water in the ocean is rising. Many lowlands are being reclaimed by the sea, as is the case in Bangladesh where every year the poor peasants are losing the land, which is the only way for them to survive.

Not too many of us are able to meditate on these possibilities since the demand of our daily life keep us busy most of the time, and some opt to ignore the whole thing because it is too confusing or because it is easier to leave everything in the hands of God. At this point, the best solution is to take it philosophically and follow the popular expression: che sarà, sarà. The truth is that the prophecy "dust will return to dust" is more than ever evident. No matter what, if you look around or think about the hardest matter on this earth, given it enough time, it will decay and will return to its original form: "dust." The only truth is that there was a beginning, and there will be an end to everything, and after that, everybody can fantasize as to what is in store for us.

CHAPTER IV

Religion and Its Role in Our Lives

Major religions

As I mentioned before, it seems that the majority of people relies on the religious authorities to make all the decisions on many topics that concerns the proper behavior and accept them as the ultimate truth while there are many others who are not convinced of the rationality of some of the rules and find their own answers. Since unity makes strength, each religion has to present a unified doctrine; otherwise, the fragmentation according to the different interpretations of the followers would destroy the religious community itself. In the past, we have the decision of King James to have an official translation of the Bible since there were so many of them that it created confusion among the believers. But this practice could also present some negative results. We have the case of the pope whose decisions are "infallible" when he speaks "ex cathedra." Most of the time when dealing with doctrinal issues, there is no problem, but sometimes, some of the decisions do not agree with the scientific or practical facts. Think of the trouble that the poor Galileo ended up because his discovery about our solar system did not agree with the preaching of the church. So if the church was wrong at times in the past, it is very possible that mistakes can be made at any other time. For this reason, it would be more advisable for the religious authorities to make suggestions rather than dictate strict rules and to allow each individual member to find his own answers so that while remaining a member, he may still be free to live according to his own beliefs. As long as human beings are involved, nothing is perfect, and chances are, mistakes will be made.

At the present time, from a religious point of view, the most argued and very moving topic which the whole society is divided is the problem of abortion, which has also become a very sensitive political issue. Regardless of religious and political affiliations, society is divided into two groups: pro-life and pro-choice. Both groups have solid rational reasons for their choice, and it is difficult for anyone who is confronted with this terrible decision to choose one or the other. The best solution is not to be caught in this situation, and if all the religions would promote and instruct people on how to prevent pregnancies, the problem would not exist. However, as always, mistakes are made, and whoever is involved has to pay a price for it. For those people who firmly believe in one or the other practice, there is no choice to be made. They know exactly what to do. The dilemma is for those who are not sure about what is the proper procedure to follow. In order to sway the undecided, one way or another, both factions come up with all sort of reasons why their way of dealing with it is the proper one. As a matter of fact, the issue had to be brought in the courts of the nation to find a proper solution. While legally there was a solution, morally the issue was not resolved and the arguments go on as ever. This proves that courts and politicians cannot solve religious and moral problems and should stay out of it.

LIFE: ITS PROBLEMS & SOME OF ITS UNANSWERABLE QUESTIONS

The "Pro Life" group comes in with a very strong and scary statement: "Abortion is the killing of a human being." Since from conception the fetus is considered a human being and no matter what is the reason, God created it, and at anytime it is eliminated it is a crime against God do so. A stronger argument cannot be made and many are in agreement with this position. On the other end the "Pro Choice" group claims that abortion is not the killing of a human being since the fetus does not have a life of his own until birth, and it is only an addendum to the mother's body. Others are in between the two and point out that if the fetus is eliminated at an early stage it should be an acceptable practice. There are also other situations to be considered. What should be done in the case of a fetus that is abnormal, or is the result of a rape, incest, or simply rejection by the parents? For the "Pro Life" group this is the will of God and man has no authority to override it. Life should go on regardless of the terrible situation. For the other group this solution is not acceptable since we are condemning a poor human being to live a life deprived since birth of all the basic pleasures that the good Lord granted the humans in order to live in accordance to His will, and in order to fulfill its destiny. In cases of this kind, it should be strictly the decision of the parents and society should only provide the necessary medical services as required regardless of the moral issues. The best way to come up with an acceptable solution is if each one of us would put himself in such a predicament and ask himself: what would I do in such situation? Would I chose to live in such condition or would a prefer death?

At this point, we have to ask ourselves: should society let life go on according to the law of nature or should Humans take control of its own growth and development? The human race does not seem to be on the verge of extinction. As a matter of fact, it seems that we are overpopulating this earth to the point that if we do not take some corrective actions we may be facing serious problems feeding the people and give them a chance to live a quality life. If the good Lord gave us "Intelligence," we must use it in controlling and improving the environment in which we live. Every day on TV, we see picture of starving children, some making a living by salvaging few scraps of material from mountains of garbage that others have discarded. We are constantly asked to make donation so their lives can be saved. Millions of dollars are donated for this purpose and only God knows how much of it reaches the poor children. So we save some of the children, but what is the quality of their future life? Would it not be better if we teach the people from underdeveloped countries to avoid bringing into this life children that they cannot adequately raise and support? In the latter case, we would not be facing the problem of starving children. Shouldn't society be concerned with the growth of its population and make sure, that it can provide a quality life to all concerned?

Even if we can feed the whole world with no problem, still we have a big problem finding a way to dispose of the waste created by it. And we have all the means necessary to eliminate these problems, the only missing factor is that not all people are aware of this situation or are not willing to do anything about it.

For centuries, there were bloody conflicts among the major religions trying to overpower each other and impose their faith all over the world, because each believed to have a mandate from God to do so. But in the Western world, with the separation of church and state and more democratic governments, even different religions were able to coexist in the same countries. Up to few years back the more common situation was that different religions were usually confined within ethnic groups living in different countries, and except for few missionaries who went around trying to convert people to their faith, life went on according to the local rules and social traditions. In recent years, political and economical necessities have forced thousands of people and entire families to move from a country to another and some of the traditional customs and ceremonies have made their way into the new countries. Some traditions and customs are confined to the place of worship and the private homes, and do not cause any concern to the other groups of different faith.

For example, there is a religious group believing that food should be processed according to some strict rules and pork should be eliminated from their diet. Some observe it to the letter while other are lukewarm about it, and many more do not play any attention to it since the rule was very practical from an health point of view in the old days, but now with the new sanitary conditions it is not necessary anymore. There is also another very important rule in another group, which prohibits its followers to have meat on Fridays. In the old days m eat was a luxury and eliminating it was considered some kind of fasting. Most of the people used fish as an alternative since in the past it was abundant and cheap. I heard some say that the true reason was because the disciples were fishermen, and Jesus wanted to give them some help and make sure that at least once a week they would have a good day in selling their catch. At present, fish has become so expensive and if we consider that shrimps, lobsters, and caviar are considered fish product, eating them cannot be considered fasting. As we can clearly see, it is strictly a personal choice and by observing these rules there is no interference with the way of living of other people. We even have the case of the Amish people who refuse to accept the use of new and more productive tools available. They have their own dress code, travel with their horses and buggies, and till the earth with tools that were used centuries ago. They don't seem to bother anybody and society leaves them alone to live according to their religious beliefs.

LIFE: ITS PROBLEMS & SOME OF ITS UNANSWERABLE QUESTIONS

In some cases, the religious practice may violate the laws of the land and conflicts have to be cleared up. In the past, we had problems with the Mormons' practice of polygamy, which was solved by outlawing it. Still, it seems that members of that religion practice it to some extent. The whole thing could be ignored since it does not directly involve the general public and the state could only recognize and give a legal status only to one marriage. However, recently it was brought to the attention of the authorities that many marriages were prearranged and in some cases against the will of the brides that turned out to be underage. In these cases, we clearly have the violation of the civil, human rights of the women involved, and there is no question that the state has to intervene to stop this illegal practice. The same attitude should be applied against those cults that practice animal sacrifices since people in the Western world do not accept cruelty against animals. In general, the separation of church and state seems to be very fair because it allows people to live according to their choices. But now and then we come across situations that put certain practices in violation of the law of the land. At this point, we have serious problems and it is not easy to find a fair solution for all concerned.

If we look at ourselves, there is no doubt that we see us made up by a double nature. On one end we see our "body" which acts independently as far as its physical growth is concerned and follows only the genetic map inherited, on the other we see our "mind" trying to keep the body and our actions under control. Nothing can go on without a functioning body, and most of our achievements will be directly related to its condition, and life, as we know it, ends when our body ceases to function. Before being able to accomplish anything, we have to make sure that our physical condition is at its best. Generally, we take for granted our good health and it is only when something goes wrong with it when we realize what our first priority is. Has anyone tried to concentrate on any mental activity while the pain from a tooth or the back or other bad body conditions forces the brain to focus only on getting rid of the pain? When the physical pain is strong enough, nothing else is relevant. There are certain demands from our body and we try to fulfill them as best as we can. We are talking about food, shelter from the elements, rest, sleep, sex, etc. We try doing it in a rational way, since if we neglect or abuse certain rules we will get sick and will not be able to perform our daily chores or if carried to extremes our body dies and life as we know it, ends there. In order to be alive and accomplish anything we have to have a functioning body, and this should be our first priority. The Roman used to say: "Mens sana in corpore sano" (Healthy mind in a healthy body). Unfortunately, for many people the physical part of their lives becomes the only reason to be alive, and they completely forget or overlook the spiritual part that make life worth living and gives us the best rewards that we could wish for. In doing so, they become selfish, greedy, and create unpleasant living conditions for the other people that have to share this planet with them.

Looking around we clearly see that not everyone is doing a good job at keeping their body at peak performance. In the majority of the cases, people try to blame the genes, since we have no control over them, but in most cases it is the individual who is not doing a good job in taking care of his body and that is why we see people who are fat, skinny, strong, weak, healthy, sick, and all others anywhere within those classifications.

Fortunately lately, even the cases of malformation or undesirable physical characteristics, can be corrected thanks to the great strides achieved in the field of plastic surgery. Many people who want and can afford it, take advantage of it, and as usual many others abuse it. Some may have seen on TV the case of the woman who went through several operations to have her face look like that of a cat, but the most common one is that of young ladies who go for breast augmentation. Some of them mistakenly believe that the "more is the better" and end up giving the impression of a cow ready to be milked, which instead of making them look sexy, makes them look ridiculous. Others use it to eliminate the sign of old age or to change their identity and at this point we ask ourselves who sets the limits and the ethical values for the surgeons who are involved in these practices and for t he sake of making a "buck" they are willing do anything people request.

And in this area we also have the problem of those people who either in the case of narcissism or to overachieve in their sport activities get involved with the use of steroids and growth hormones which has been proven to be very detrimental to the well-being of the persons involved. And once more we can clearly see that even things that are good for you can be stretched to a point when they become harmful when misused. Unfortunately, what used to be "let the best person win" has become "you most win at any cost." The idea of "playing the best you can" and "act as a gentlemen" which was what sports were all about, has become obsolete, because the greed for popularity and financial gains supersede any other moral value. And even if there is no financial reward, for self-serving reasons, many activities force ambitious people seeking fame and notoriety to engage in very dangerous activities, such mountain climbing, exploration of caves and jungles, scuba diving, speed records, etc., that in many cases go array and require the intervention of public safety personnel at great expenses for the community involved, and even when they have positive results do not bring any practical and useful advantage for the progress of the humanity. And since we are on the topic of useless and potentially harmful social activities, we can mention all sorts of other contests such as the record for "the most hot dogs, or pies, or other foods" eaten in a certain period of time when people push their limits and create a disgusting scene rather than an entertaining one. But as we say in English to "each his own" and the Roman: "De gustibus no est disputandum" we have to accept a certain amount of strange behavior as long as it does not surpass certain limits, but who sets the limits?

After having satisfied our physical needs, only then we can focus on our emotional, intellectual, and spiritual needs. Our mind or our soul seems to be in charge of decision-making and providing guidance to all our actions. With our mind, we make decision that control the actions that our body performs and we are always seeking some rational explanation to justify the way we behave. When dealing with our physical needs most of the time there are natural guidelines to go by, but when we are dealing with ethical and moral questions, it becomes difficult because we have to rely for guidance on the sum of our experiences, education, and indoctrination received, which invariably is different from one individual to another. While many of these actions are dictated by the legal systems of each nation, many others are dictated by the religious beliefs of the individuals, and there begins the struggle to live the "right" way in order to obtain the proper rewards in the afterlife.

Pilgrimage to Mecca

In general, while almost all people claim to belong to some sort of religious denomination, very few people live strictly by those rules. Many practice their faith as if it was more of a traditional way of life than a strong need to serve the Lord, and while many go to the church of their choice on Sunday, for many of them it is only a day off from work. There is no question that in our daily life our physicals and social needs get all of our attention and our spiritual life takes second place. It is only when there is a crisis and a person desperately needs help or in more serious cases life itself is at stake that people turn to God asking for His help. It is at this point that we have a wide variety of results and different interpretations of the facts.

When there are no positive results it seems that, our prayers went unanswered and some people feel that they were not "good" enough to deserve a special consideration. In case there is a positive result some may consider it a mere coincidence, others an unexplainable phenomenon, and for some other strong believers it is a "miracle." Since there is no rational explanation, no one can argue to prove an acceptable point of view. But for the people who consider it a miracle, a question should come up for an explanation. Assuming that all the people asking for help were equally "good," then why some would be granted their wishes and others would not. It is true that if all good people would be granted special treatment only on the ground of being "good" then by now all humans would have caught up with it and everybody would be good and get all their wishes fulfilled, and the purpose of our life on earth as we know it, would have no meaning. But then the question still remains: why God would help some good people and not all of them? It is true that we are not capable of understanding the way God operates, but by any standards if that were the case he would appear to be very unfair.

Many people in addition to the Divine Intervention seek the help of Saints and or close relatives that have passed on. The situation is still the same, and we would have to believe that especially in the case of a relative that could be a loving parent or another close member of the family, if there was a way, all our wishes would be fulfilled in no time. The truth is that we in no way can establish any link to the life after death. It is only faith, hope and the belief that there must be something after the end of our physical life, and we will find out only when we die. We can only speculate that our afterlife can be visualized and understood as we do with dreams. Everything we do while dreaming is done without any physical part of the body. Everything is mental but we do things and act the same as when we are awake. So we can assume that life can go on at a spiritual level since the body is made up of matter that has a limited lifetime and that after a certain amount of time dies and decays. In view of this fact we have to conclude that our physical body has no place in the afterlife, and it is not rationally viable to accept the resurrection of the body, nor the physical rewards in the afterlife such as the "land of milk and honey" or "the seventy virgins" at your disposal and other gifts that in our normal daily life on this earth would be very attractive rewards. However, since God is omnipotent, there is no way for us to limit is actions to what we think is reasonable or not, and anything that comes to anyone's imagination is a feasible possibility if he is willing to do so. For example, there is no way to accept and deny the fact that in rewarding and punishing anybody's behavior in this life he could use a physical way of doing so. From our human point of view we can accept the fact that if a rich person did not use his wealth properly, a just punishment would be to make him return to life in this world or in a parallel one since there may be millions of them in the universe, as a poor person struggling to make a living. On the contrary, if a person struggled all his life to make a living, but lived according to very moral and ethical values he could be rewarded with a new life, which would fulfill all his wishes and desires. This "law of the opposite" could be applied to reward or punish any kind of behavior of all human beings. It may sound as fair practice, but it is only a product of our imagination.

Giotto (the Last Judgment)

CHAPTER V

The Human Race

From the private collection of Len Forrest
(Old Field, New York-Boca Raton, Florida)

To further complicate things, the good Lord decided to divide the human beings into different ethnic groups. Many believe that it was part of the evolution of the world. They say that time, isolation, climate, food, etc., gave each group different external appearance. Not too many people would accept this explanation, and the majority doesn't seem to have any rational answers for it. The fact is that all of us have to face this reality, and in so doing, many problems come up, and each one of us has to find a solution of his own. In the old days, the races were kept separate by the geographical boundaries and physical barriers, however, at the present time, the means of transportation and the need for trade have eliminated these limits; and the races have come in contact with each other, and as expected, many problems have developed. A brief review of world history reveals that in several parts of the world, great civilizations of different ethnic groups have existed and made tremendous progress in many areas of the human knowledge such as engineering, astronomy, mathematics, agriculture, etc., but at a certain point for one reason or another, they ceased to exist or lost their power and influence and did not have an active part in the evolution of the modern world. The only civilization that was able to survive was the one that from the great Greek period, which was absorbed by the Roman one, and developed into what became the Western civilization, which for a while took control of the rest of the world.

From the private collection of Len Forrest
(Old Field, New York-Boca Raton, Florida)

The fact is that the stronger and more evolved civilizations took advantage of the more primitive ones, and for the past several centuries, we have seen the Europeans having a superior role in the world affairs and using the people from the underdeveloped nations to their own advantage. For many years, people from underdeveloped countries provided a good source of cheap labor, and as history tells us, in many instances, they were uprooted from their villages and sold into slavery. This was an acceptable practice as long as we can remember throughout the world history. It was so profitable for the people in control that there was no attempt to change the "status quo" until recently. Now we have the people from the third world trying to catch up and take advantage of the progress that humans have made in the last few centuries. But the process is slow and difficult, and many nations are having difficulties in keeping their citizens from starving, never mind giving them a proper education and better living standards. Some of the people are so desperate that they will do anything to move into more advanced societies, and in many cases, they risk their lives so that they may have a chance to improve their living conditions and provide a better future for their children. Since most of them lack education or training, they have no choice but to accept any jobs that no one else wants, or that pay very little, so their living standards are way below the average ones. All of them come from different ethnic groups, mostly nonwhite. The latest estimates indicate that in the United States at the present time, there are eleven millions illegal immigrants who come pouring in from our open borders seeking a better way to make a living. The same is happening in Europe. In addition to those who manage to get through the borders on land, there are thousands who, from the coast of North Africa, risk their lives to cross the Mediterranean Sea on some boats that can barely stay afloat, and in many cases, they sink causing the death of thousands of desperate people. These migrations cause many problems of moral nature. Should those who have more, share it with those who don't have anything? Is it right to see people dying of starvation while others have no problems of this nature? Many people feel that society should do its best to help these people in distress, and undoubtedly, that is the way to go, but the problem is so big that cannot be solved in any simple way. Society faces the same problem a captain in a rescue boat that can safely hold only ten people, and there are twenty to be rescued. Should he try to save all of them and run the risk of causing the death of everyone or save only ten and let the rest die?

From the private collection of Len Forrest
(Old Field, New York-Boca Raton, Florida)

LIFE: ITS PROBLEMS & SOME OF ITS UNANSWERABLE QUESTIONS

The influx of these unfortunate human beings in more advanced civilized societies creates a class of underprivileged and uneducated people that some consider lazy, less intelligent than normal people and, therefore, deserve to live in their below standards conditions. On the opposite side, among the minority groups, there is a strong belief that there is a great deal of discrimination against people of color, so they think that no matter how hard they try, they will never be able to reach the same objectives as the whites. There may be some apparent good points in both arguments, but both are wrong. Human beings are all the same. It is true that the physical appearance may be different, and there is no scientific explanation for its origins even though we know that the genes in our body decide our physical appearance. Still, we don't know how and why they came into existence. We are aware that the body tries to develop itself according to the needs of the individual person. Those who require a great amount of physical work usually develop strong muscles to facilitate their manual jobs, and those who are required to use their mental abilities in the long run acquire better mental skills to help them deal in a better way the demands of their jobs. This process has nothing to do with intelligence. Even the famous IQ test is not a very good measurement of a person's intelligence, since it measures only certain skills that

From the private collection of Len Forrest
(Old Field, New York-Boca Raton, Florida)

one acquires simply by living in special social groups. Gyms are becoming very popular for people who want to improve their physical health and strength, and so school with good educational standards are the best means to improve a person's intellectual capacities. All other arguments have no value. Accordingly, we clearly see that at the present time all modern societies have recognized that all men are equal, and all people know that talents and hard work will always bring in the desired results. Marketable talents always bring in financial rewards regardless of the color and the races of the individual involved. It is true that some racial and ethnic discrimination may still exist at a personal level, but on the national level, that excuse is no longer acceptable. In any modern society, everybody has the same chance to learn and develop his own talents in order to live a decent and prosperous life.

One of the most serious problems that we have at the present time is the world's overpopulation. In the past centuries, famine, plague, wars, and other world's disasters along with the poor medical conditions kept the population down. Now with modern technology, we have been able to eliminate these problems, but at the same time, we are creating more serious ones. In order to meet the needs of the people, we have to produce more goods, and to produce more goods, we need more people; and this cycle goes on and on to the point that natural resources are getting depleted and eventually will run out. In addition, we are having serious problems disposing of our waste material, and we are creating so much pollution that, in turn, contributes to the global warming that eventually will melt the glaciers at the poles with the flooding of the lowlands and so on and on. It is time that we should seriously consider controlling the increase of the world's population and make sure that our resources grow accordingly so that we can take care adequately of the needs of all the people on this earth. It is true that some day we may be able to colonize some other planet out there in space, but for the present time, we have not developed a way to do so, and accordingly, we have to live within our means.

CHAPTER VI

The Individual Human Being

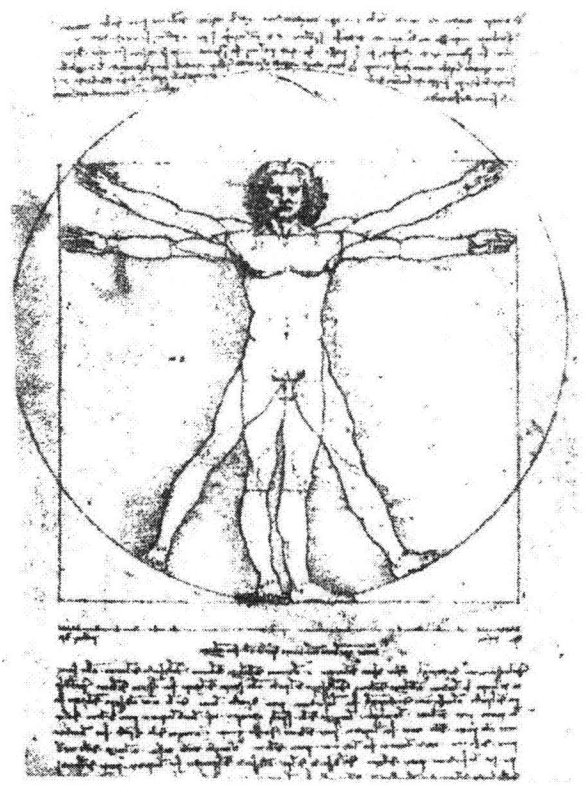

The human anatomy

Billions of people live on this planet, and their presence make it the way it is. Each person is different from any other one, and while we know all about genes, DNA, and fertilization, no one can explain to us why we are born of a certain sex, from certain parents, and in a particular location. Nobody can recall being asked or having a choice about the infinite possibilities that we have. It is difficult to accept the fact that some people are so "proud "of what they are. It sounds like they did something to deserve what they received in terms of parents, family, country, and physical appearance. I am sure that many would like to change some of these traits for the ones of their choices.

In the beginning of our lives, our main concern is the physical well-being, which is provided by our parents and which creates a bond between them and us. But as we grow up, we become aware of ourselves and the world around us. Our body and our physical appearance is our first experience. Some people are well endowed and are very happy about their body while others are not and feel that Mother Nature was not very kind with them. This is one of the most critical points of our lives. Many accept themselves for what they are and try to improve on it while others go through life resenting the fact that they are not what they would have liked to be, and this resentment undermines any future achievement. Later on, we take a closer look at our parents. Their intellectual and physical conditions, and their social status is also a very important factor in a child future life, and their acceptance is also vital in the formation of the future person. There is an infinity of variations from one individual to another, both physical and mental, and each one of us has a place somewhere on that human scale. Most of the people try their best to improve both the physical and mental capabilities, and the results vary according to the abilities and efforts of each individual. As it is commonly said, it is "the sum of our experiences" that will dictate what we will become.

During his lifetime, an individual goes through several stages. Each one is very important in the development of the person, who will be influenced by the experience received during each one of them. From infancy, one goes into childhood years, and perhaps these are the most beautiful years in the life of a human being. There are no demands, no decisions to be made, and no pressures from any source; and the child grows surrounded by love and affection, and everything needed is provided for him. He tries to be whatever his parents want him to be, and in general, he does his best to imitate them. It is at this very stage that everything surrounding the child leaves an indelible mark on his psyche. He will forever remember every inch of his physical birthplace, the food that he craved to satisfy his hunger, the familiar faces that were always around him, the panoramic visions of the town in which he lived—and no matter what for the rest of his life, these happy images will bring back a great nostalgia for the "back home" syndrome. For as long as the person lives, he will always have a preference for the mountains or the seashore or the metropolitan way of living and the special food that he got accustomed to eat and the games played according to what is deeply imprinted in his memory, and he will be always bragging about the fact that those were the best years of his life that in many cases do not exist anymore except in a deep, remote corner of his memory.

The next stage is more difficult because the child goes into adolescence, and with the hormones and the "self" setting in, there is a strong need to assert oneself as a person; and the individual has to learn how to deal with his own sexuality and people around him. Also at this time, one finds out what his limitations and potentials are and prepares himself to face the future by getting the best possible training and education. At the next stage, as a young person, everyone has to make very important decision about the various possible social venues that are available in order to make the best possible living in the future years. Any wrong decision at this time may force the person to live the rest of his life doing some undesirable trade or profession, constantly repeating to himself the very common expressions "I should have" or "I could have."

Finally, having reached maturity, the person has to make another important decision that is also vital to the success of his future life. Now is the time to start a family. The choices of companions are unlimited, but not everybody is lucky enough to make the best choice. Again, if a wrong choice is made, the consequences will be felt for the rest of one's life. It is at this time of life that a person can stand back and enjoy the fruits of the past hard work and struggles, provided all the right decisions were made. With a nice house, a loving family, an interesting job, and a decent salary, one can consider himself very lucky; and this period probably is the best and the longest of a person's life. It is a great feeling to see children grow up, repeating the cycle of life. And with the arrival of the grandchildren, more joy and warmth is added to the family life, which at this point on the horizon has for the grandparents the lure of the golden years of retirement. It sounds like a fairy tale, but for sure, many people are blessed with a life like this, or at least very close to it.

Going back to the beginning of life, the reality is that many people are not lucky enough to have loving parents, if any. Many others do not handle very well their adolescent years, and without good counseling, they strive for wrong goals and make many mistakes that will have dire consequences on their future lives. And even when a person has managed to go through these years very well, a wrong choice of job or companion can make life a very miserable experience. Up to this point, it has been a person's choice to make the right decisions. But when it comes to children, no one has anything do with their physical and mental conditions. They come as they are, and we have to do the best to bring them up, and sometimes even after a very loving and careful upbringing, they may not measure up to the expectations that every parent has hoped for. Fortunately, in the last few years, research in this field shows hopes that we may have some control over their gender, and with the genes' and DNA's therapies improve the physical and mental qualities of the newborn.

This process reflects the development of fairly normal persons. How about the life of those people that for some reason or another are physically handicapped from birth? Nobody wants this to happen, but it is a reality, and we have to face this terrible situation. In extreme cases, the person from birth is condemned to live a miserable life with no hope for improvement in the future. Yes, we have the obligation to support the unfortunate human being in any possible way, but do we have the right to force this person to live in those conditions? Should he have the right to terminate his life, or should his parents make the decision to prevent him to be born in the first place? Each one of us could come up with a different answer, but which one is the right one?

Then we have the case of those persons that physically appear to be normal, but internally, the body is not working according to the norm. In some cases, these problems are created by physical abnormality; in others, these may be induced by psychological reasons. In the past, they were forced to keep their handicap a secret because society did not understand their abnormality and did not accept their lifestyle. Lately, society has been able to understand their predicament and the majority of the people has accepted their behavior, but in many cases, there is nothing that can be done to change their conditions, society leaves them alone to live their lives the best way they can. But some of them claim that it is only their choice of lifestyle, and since all men are created equal and have the same rights, they should be considered normal people and publicly engage in their lifestyle and go as far as to demand that a regular marriage contract should be allowed to two people of the same sex. Some people graciously go along with these demands, but it seems that the majority is not very comfortable with it. The truth is that many people feel a very strong revulsion in being exposed to this type of behavior and consequently do not wish it to be forced on them as a part of an acceptable lifestyle in their communities. It is as if someone would be picking his nose or taking care of some private bodily function in front of you. There is the proper time, the proper place, and the proper way to do anything, and other people's feeling always must be taken into consideration. The truth is that the old generation has more difficulty in accepting changes in their social behavior while the young one is open to accept new and different ways of life.

All through the different stages of life, people are aware of our dual makeup. There is always the dialogue between the body and the "self." In many ways, we have complete control of our body, and we can do with it whatever we want; but in others, we have no control over it. It has a development of its own, and at the present time, we have some power to make some significant changes, but not a complete control of it. It has a clock of its own, and so far, we have not been able to find out how it works. Our body goes through the different changes from birth to death, and although we may delay or make few cosmetic changes, ultimately it reaches the end of its cycle. We all know what happens to our body, but so far, no one has been able to show in a rational and undeniable terms what happens to the *self* that is commonly called the *soul*. We have many episodes of people who were declared legally dead and then came back to life. We heard about their experiences with the "lights" and their flying around and observing the physical world, but nothing is very rational and conclusive enough to explain what is waiting for us after death.

As mentioned before, there are people who don't believe in anything, and for them, when a person dies, that is the end of everything. On the other end, there are those who strongly believe in their religion, and for them, the good Lord has planned a rewarding experience after death. There have been speculations about this reward or punishment through the centuries, but no one knows for sure what it is. In the middle, there are those people who would like to believe, but they need a more rational explanation in order to accept the religious view. Even in the case of those who, in their early years, were exposed to a strong religious indoctrination, later on in life, doubts may come up. This process is almost the same as the one children go through with the fairy tales. In their infancy, they believe them to be true, but as they grow up, they become more skeptical in accepting them as facts. Each individual is exposed to different kinds of life experiences, and some of them have no rational explanations. For many, it is the will of God, and they accept it without questions. Others talk about bad or good luck, and finally, there are those who believe it is fate. But can anyone explain what is *luck* or what is *fate* and who makes the decisions and is in control of them?

In many cases, individuals establish direct dialogue with God and firmly believe that if they obey all the divine laws everything will turn out good for them. Sometimes, everything goes well, and there is no problem; however, in many cases, some bad things happen. And the person is startled and cannot understand why this has happened, so there are some who accept it philosophically as the will of God, and others cry out, "God why me? What have I done wrong?" The same situation occurs when people try to barter with God: "Good Lord, if you do this for me, I promise I will do . . . for you." In some cases, the wish is granted, and the person is convinced that God has answered his prayers. But in many cases, the wishes do not come through, and the person cannot make any sense of why the prayers went unanswered since the good Lord is supposed to be a loving being, always ready to help us in case of difficulties. For many people, God is supposed to be a personal "genie" ready to come to our aid anytime we need him, but unfortunately, that is not the case, and everyone reacts to it in different ways. Worst of all is when things of real cruel and inhuman nature involving innocent people happen. That is when all people cry out, "Lord, how can you allow things like this to happen?" But there is no answer or any explanation for it.

The dialogue is only a one-way discussion, which is no dialogue at all. We all have lost close friends and members of the family, and during their lifetime, all of them would have done anything to come to our aid in times of crisis. But no matter what we do, there is no response from them. We ask ourselves, "Where are they? Why can't they do something for us?" But there is no explanation for it. There are times when we could consider a favorable resolution of a crisis, an intervention from a loved one that we have turned to for help, but there is no tangible evidence that such is the case; therefore, most of the people consider it a coincidence rather than a miracle. So while we can come up with an infinity of conjectures about life after death for most people, there are no answers, and only those who have faith in their religion seem to have them. According to human expectations, those who do good should get a reward, and those who act poorly should be punished. But looking around, it seems that in general that principle does not work during this life. Sometimes, we see good people struggling and facing all kinds of hardship, and bad people having an easy time and enjoying a good life. No one can make any sense out of it, and each person interprets the situation in his own way, but in many cases, it may weaken the faith that some people have in the divine justice.

No matter what we believe, it seems that in general, nobody feels at easy with the thought of dying. Except the case of desperate people for whom life is not worth living anymore, or some other people who are experiencing extreme physical or mental pain, just about everybody puts up a good fight to stay alive as long as possible. It does not make any sense, especially in the case of people who strongly believe that they will be rewarded in the afterlife with whatever they expect from the Lord. Accordingly, it should be that they would be looking forward to such an event, but there are very few of such cases; the rest seems to be uneasy or uncomfortable with it, and every death is a sad event and is mourned by the living. The only truth is that there is no escape from it, we all have a date for it, and sooner or later, we all have to face it and find out for ourselves what is it all about.

The best way to face death is when the individual has no guilty feelings, and this feeling is also a great help in order to have a good and peaceful life. When a person knowingly does something wrong, it is inevitable that a guilty feeling will set in his conscience, and sooner or later, it will come up and haunt him. There is always fear that somehow some kind of punishment will be coming, and especially facing death, this guilty feeling could be extremely uncomfortable, to say the least. But if a person in all his life has tried to the best of his knowledge to do the right things and bought no harm to anybody, this person not only will have a happy and serene life, but will not be worried about death or any other circumstance that he may face anytime, anywhere. Facing the end of life on this planet, one has to be proud of his accomplishments or at least feel that he did the best according to his abilities and have no regrets or having guilty feelings for pursuing the wrong goals. Life could be much more pleasant if everyone would live by this principle.

Recently, I overheard a person telling a joke about a man that according to his doctor had only few more months to live. He went to church and begged the good Lord to cure him of this disease and give him a chance to live a longer life. He said, "Lord, all my life I have been a good and honest person. I never drank alcohol, never chased women, never smoked, never ate fancy food or more than I should have, I did not squander money on vacations or other unnecessary luxuries, and I always worked very hard, and you should let me live longer." And the Lord replied, "My good man, if what you are telling me is the truth, I don't understand what in the world you want to live for!"

OBSERVATIONS I

Once at the beginning of the sermon, the pastor asked the congregation, "How many of you are unhappy?" Some of the people raised their hands. Then he asked, "How many are happy?" A larger number raised their hands. "You are all lying," remarked the pastor. I was taken back by his remark, and somehow, I missed his explanation because I was also trying to explain to myself what makes a person happy. The first thing that came to my mind was that if someone was rich enough, he could be happy. But that is not enough because if a person does not have good health, he can be very miserable. So let him have good health and riches. Is this enough? No, a person needs love, friendship, family, etc. So let him have all of the above. At this point, we have to take a look at him. Is he tall, short, fat, skinny, intelligent, good looking, etc.? Even though the situation is quite impossible that a person may have all of these good qualities, he may not be happy with his race, nationality, or the place where he lives. And we can go on bringing up factors which could ruin the happiness of a person. Also, an important factor in the consideration of any of these positive qualities is the extent—or better yet—the level of the same. If you are strong, intelligent, handsome, etc., and even if you are at the highest level in one category, you may not be at the same level in another. It is evident that the possession of any or all of these desirable qualities do not guarantee happiness. So what is the answer to our question "are you happy"?

In our daily life, when we look around, we always find happy and sad people in all sorts of situations: economic, ethnic, physical appearance, national origin, etc. We can find happy and unhappy people in the exact social, physical, and economic situation. So how can we explain the different attitudes of people in general? If we take a closer look at ourselves, we find out that we have little to do with what we are. We may have a lot to do with what we become. I don't remember anyone asking me where would I have liked to be born, from which parents, male or female, tall or short, white of colored, intelligent or not, etc. All I know is that I found myself in this world, born in a certain place, from some unknown parents, and having a body that may or not be the way I would like it to be. Do I take credit and brag for what I am if I consider myself lucky for my good fortune? Or is it my fault for being born in a bad situation? Should I feel guilty or embarrassed for what I am?

The way we answer the above questions may be the key to our happiness. It seems that life is like a theatrical production. There is a cast, and each person has no choice but to play the role assigned to him/her. One may have a better role than another, but we have no input in determining it. Either one accepts the role assigned or does not. From the professional point of view, it is not the part that we play, but how well we play it. Hence, the answer to our question: in life, it is not the nature of our assigned part to play, but how well we play that part. The secret is in the acceptance of our state of being, and how well we use our natural talents to improve that condition. The degree of our happiness is directly related to how we accept our situation, and how well we perform.

Dance Like No One's Watching

We convince ourselves that life will be better after we get married, have a baby, then another. Then we are frustrated that the kids aren't old enough, and we'll be more content when they are. After that, we're frustrated that we have teenagers to deal with. We will certainly be happy when they are out of that stage. We tell ourselves that our life will be complete when our spouse gets his or her act together, when we get a nicer car, are able to go on a nice vacation, and when we retire.

The truth is, there's no better time to be happy than right now. If not now, when? Your life will always be filled with challenges. It's best to admit this to yourself and decide to be happy anyway.

One of my favorite quotes comes from Alfred D. Souza. He said, "For a long time it had seemed to me that life was about to begin—real life. But there was always some obstacle in the way, something to be gotten through first, some unfinished business, time still to be served, a debt to be paid. Then life would begin. At last it dawned on me that these obstacles were my life."

This perspective has helped me to see that there is no way to happiness. Happiness is the way. So treasure every moment that you have. And treasure it more because you shared it with someone special, special enough to spend your time. And remember that time waits for no one.

So stop waiting until you finish school, until you go back to school, until you lose ten pounds, until you gain ten pounds, until you have kids, until your kids leave the house, until you start work, until you retire, until you get married, until you get divorced, until Friday night, until Sunday morning, until you get a new car or home, until your car or home is paid off, until spring, until summer, until fall, until winter, until you are off welfare, until the first or fifteenth, until your song comes on, until you've had a drink, until you've sobered up, until you die, until you are born again to decide that there is no better time than right now to be happy. Happiness is a journey, not a destination.

> Thought for the day:
> Work like you don't need money,
> Love like you've never been hurt,
> And dance like no one's watching.
>
> —Anonymous

CHAPTER VII

Nationality

The United Nations building

As far as anyone knows, the good Lord did not divide the earth into different nations among people of different races and different languages. In the very beginning, people roamed around alone, trying to find food and shelter. After a while they discovered that unity gave them more power, and the more the number of people involved, the easier was to obtain some desired results. In many cases, it was impossible to survive without the help of other people, so they had no choice but to stick together. From the basic family units came the tribes, and several of them formed villages, which evolved into cities; and from their union, the entire nations were created. These changes were not always dictated by the needs, but most of the time, greed was involved. The stronger people took advantage of the weaker ones, took over their fertile lands, and enjoyed the fruits of their labor as long as they could. These conditions could not go on unchallenged, and fighting always erupted among the oppressors and the oppressed; therefore war, whether defensive or offensive, became an integral part of human life on this planet.

From the known history of the world, we can see that many nations and some great leaders tried on several occasion to unite the different civilizations under one nation, but they did not last very long. The only one that succeeded in such endeavor for a considerable amount of time was the Roman Empire. After centuries of wars, finally the Romans were able to conquer all the known world of their time and enjoy the famous *Pax Romana* that lasted over three centuries. One of the reasons for their success was that once they took over another nation, they made sure that its people became Roman citizens with equal rights and sharing of all the advantages of their advanced civilization. During this period, there were no wars, and people were able to engage in the development of all sorts of engineering, architecture, arts, commerce, and other forms of sophisticated living. It is unfortunate that they were not able to handle all that good and easy living, As the saying goes, "power corrupts." After so many years, society became so lazy, selfish, and depraved that it could not any longer survive under the pressure from the barbaric tribes, who could not resist the lure of taking possession of all the riches that were available to them, since there was no one willing to fight them. The whole civilized world came apart and was almost destroyed. For many years during the Dark Ages, civilization lost all the progress that had achieved during the golden age of the Roman Empire. From that time on, the world has been in a continuous turmoil with wars, and the destruction and creation of many nations have been the main events in the life of the present world. Many attempts were made to recreate the empire, but the people had divided into regional groups with their own languages and customs, and they had set up certain borders to their lands. Their only goal was to expand these borders as much as possible at the expense of their neighbors. The most important and almost successful attempt to bring Europe into one entity was made by Napoleon. With the excuse of bringing liberty to all oppressed people, he tried to conquer all the different countries of Europe that at that time were under brutal and oppressive monarchies. He almost succeeded, but power and the need for glory made him pursue a course of actions that brought his dreams to an end. The futile attempt to conquer Russia and the disastrous loss of four hundred thousand men put a final nail to his coffin, and that was the end of a good opportunity to bring all of Europe into one great family of people and nations. Another great opportunity was lost at the end of World War I. The League of Nations was set up to resolve peacefully any disputes that might arise among them. But since the United States did not join, it had very little political value. Also, at the end of the war, Germany tried to obtain a peace treaty on the basis of the Fourteen Points proposed by President Woodrow Wilson, but the greed for land and colonies made the winning nations imposed the harsh conditions of the Treaty of Versailles (1919) in a country that had been devastated by war and was suffering with rampant inflation and high unemployment. Naturally, this situation favored the establishment of the dictatorship of Adolph Hitler who immediately set about rebuilding the army and expanding Germany's borders. Here, we have another attempt by an insane madman to conquer the world so that the supreme race, the Arian, could dominate all the inferior races on this planet.

People were shocked by the horrors of this cruel and unnecessary war that had taken the lives of millions of innocent people and destroyed entire countries, so in 1945, the United Nations was founded. There was a strong determination on the part of the international communities that no more wars should ever occur. No sooner that it went into action, here we have another insane dictator: Stalin. He decided to bring the world together for the benefit of the abused masses, and in order to achieve his goal, he did not hesitate to use all sorts of tortures, assassinations, slave camps, famine, and any other means to convince people to follow his leadership. Fortunately, the human race is resilient to all these calamities and that attempt was also brought to an end by its own impracticability.

For some reason, the United Nations has managed to survive, and in spite of the corruption and inefficiency of most of its people, somehow it brings the leaders of the different nations to a dialogue that in many cases has avoided serious conflicts. It is not perfect because each member seeks to protect his own interests at the expense of other nations, but at least gives people a chance to talk about the conflicting issues that arise around the world. A more interesting and hopeful system is in existence in Europe, and it seems to be more effective in bringing together people of different nations. By eliminating the actual borders and allowing people to move around within the countries that make up the European community, there is no more reason to fight over some piece of real estate, and people can look for better financial opportunities in different places as they please.

It is a sad spectacle to see people killing each other and using death and destruction for the simple reason of different religion, nationality, and ethnic origins, such as the present situation of Kosovo, Darfur in the Sudan, and the never-ending bloody conflict between Israel and Palestine. We all know that unnecessary loss of a son, husband, brother, friend causes the same deep pain to their relatives regardless of their nationality, but the parties involved seemed to be oblivious to the terrible pains that they are imposing on other human beings for the simple "pride and devotion" to their national race, religion, and heritage. If they had sat down at a table and discussed all the existing problems, at this time all the people involved, in many cases against their will, would be enjoying the state of well-being that peace and prosperity brings to a nation. As in the litigations that come up in the civil courts of civilized countries, most of the time, people do not received 100 percent satisfaction on their desired outcome, but even if there is some loss, it is justified by the fact that there is no violence and loss of life, and the judgment is based on the best possible solution dictated by the situation.

If we take a closer look at the conflict in the Middle East, we can clearly see the negative results that pride, nationality, land, and religion can bring to millions of people that happen to be involved in it without their desire to be part of it. All the hardships that they are suffering are being imposed upon them by their leaders in the name of national pride. At this point, it is superfluous and unnecessary to discuss the legality and the reasons why the state of Israel came about to be. The fact is that, it has been in existence for over half century, it has established itself as a civilized and productive country providing its citizens with above-average quality of life. To destroy or to eliminate it from the face of the earth as it is demanded by several Arab states along its borders would mean the killing and displacement of several additional millions of innocent people who had nothing to do with its establishment or the poor living standards that exist in the surrounding states. During the various attempts to destroy this small country, the Arabs lost some additional territory that Israel kept to establish a buffer zone to better protect its inhabitants from the continuous attacks from the enemy. Now they want it back and have used this excuse as an additional reason to stage the holy war for the liberation of Palestine. The international community, unwilling to antagonize the Arabs, has taken no concrete steps to solve the situation. Every day, Israel is under attack with mortars, suicide bombers, sniper fires, and any other lethal weapons that the Arabs can devise to bring death and destruction to its people. The cry that was all over the world after WWII: *never again*! has been forgotten. There is very little reaction on the international level, but as soon as some reaction is taken by Israel to alleviate this situation, the whole world condemns these acts of violence against innocent people and considers them an overreaction. Only the United States has had the courage to become an impartial intermediary between the two fighting parties. But it seems that the

Arab countries do not want an impartial intermediary, but somebody that would side with them in obtaining the desired goals. So now the Americans are the most hated people in the Middle East, and the "holy war" has also been directed toward the destruction of our country.

The only hope we have to eliminate all these inexcusable waste of human lives and financial resources and bring much-needed help and improvements especially in some very poor countries rests with the United Nations. It is a shame that even some advanced nations use self-interest policies instead of fairness and justice for all people. A clear example of this behavior came up with the tentative of the international community to stop Saddam Hussein from causing so much chaos and destruction in the Middle East. Since they were getting cheap oil from the dictator and making huge profits from this illegal operation, France, Russia, and Germany did not care that the criminal was stealing money, which had been earmarked for buying food and medicine for his people. The results of this immoral conduct prevented the United Nations to implement the numerous resolutions enacted to stop or control the illegal practices of the dictator. This course of action led us in the unpopular war with Iraq with the relative destruction of that country, and the unnecessary deaths of so many innocent people.

And when it comes to territorial claims by some nation, it should be up to the people living on that land to decide to accept or reject the claim, and if all the rest of the civilized world would support the decision of the people involved, then there would be no wars, insurgencies, and violence in those areas. And in this case, we can refer to the uncalled and unnecessary war that Argentina waged against England for the annexation of the Falkland Islands where the mainly English population preferred to be under the rule of the British government. What a waste of lives and financial resources that could have helped the people of Argentina improve their living standards!

The same policy should be applied even when there is disagreement within the same nations, and groups of insurgents take up arms and cause death and destruction of innocent people. With the intervention of the international community or tribunal, all these disagreements within the same country could be dealt with in a fair and just way, and people could enjoy life in the pursuit of happiness, instead of killing each other. This international-supported policy could only become a reality only if we could get all nations to live up to a minimum standard of morality and ethical values. Such is the situation in Sudan with its genocide policy in the province of Darfur. Any attempt by the United Nations to send troops in the region has been stopped by Russia and China. The former has the same kind of problem in one of its province and does not want to admit any wrongdoing in repressing the rebels by any means, and the latter has made huge investments in that country and wants to keep good relations with the government in charge at the expense of the people who are suffering tremendous unjustified abuses. Once more, we see that greed, selfishness, and lack of moral character take priority over human suffering. And to make things worst, the inability of the United Nations to intervene and correct the situation encourages other despots to go on the rampage in their own countries since they feel certain that nobody will do anything to stop them. This is the current situation in Zimbabwe under the rule of Robert Mugabe. This senile eighty-four-year-old president has vowed that "only God can remove him from power." Therefore, instead of having regular elections, he went on to kill and scare the supporters of his political rival so that for sure he could win the elections. Once more, Russia and China opposed any plans by the United Nations to correct the situation.

At this time, it is evident that while in the beginning of the civilized world, *nationality* was a very important tool necessary to keep the inhabitants of a certain region safe from the possible abuses from other neighboring people. Now, its role is not that important. Many countries cannot provide its people the basic necessities of life, and people are willing to sacrifice their nationality for a chance to make a better living for themselves and their families in another country. This world was created so all people of all nationalities, races, and religions could enjoy them without any limitations from anybody. Let's hope that the movement initiated by the European community may prove to be very successful, and that it may be adopted in other locations around the world so that all those fights about borders and the takeover of land from neighboring countries may be eliminated, and people would be able to enjoy life to the fullest, instead of wasting it in the fight for additional real estate.

CHAPTER VIII

Government

The White House

As far back as we can go in the history of our world, we can see that human beings recognized the importance of the communal system in which all talents and skills of different members are used for the good of the whole community, and in exchange for some personal limitations, the individual can enjoy safety and receive all sorts of assistance in keeping a certain standard of living. The primary goal of any civilized community is to provide shelter, food, and health services to all of its members without any reservation—and these are the ingredients of the basic human rights. One of the earliest and most important forms of government in the past was theocracy, such as the one that existed for many years in Egypt. The pharaoh was considered God, and as such, he had all kinds of powers and ruled his people any way he wanted. We don't know how he became god, but we can speculate that one of the ancestors must have done some extraordinary feats for which he and his descendants assumed that position for several centuries. We had more rational forms of government during the great Hellenic Civilization during which oligarchy and democracy were introduced. Oligarchy was the easiest form of government since few people on the basis of their strength or wisdom told the rest of the countrymen what to do. This system worked quite well until the general public became more educated and affluent and demanded to have something to say in the government of the nation, so democracy was born. Unfortunately, Socrates (468-399 BC) did not like either one because the aristocrats most of the time received their position by virtue of their birthrights, and the democrats ruled by virtue of the numbers and not all people in the majority had the same amount of knowledge and wisdom. His position did not do him any good since with no friends to take his side he was condemned to death, and as I mentioned before, he had to drink his poison, which he did with a smile on his face since he firmly believed to be right in his teaching. His disciple Plato (427-348 BC) had better luck. In his book *The Republic,* he divided society in several castes, each with its own role, but it was very complicated and difficult to put into action, and it remained only one of his good ideas, which were the basis of his philosophy.

The Romans came up with another political position: emperor, which also claimed to be god, and Virgil (70-19 BC) in order to prove its veracity went through a great deal of research to write the poem "Aeneid," in which he traces the origin of the Emperor Augustus to the gods. It lasted for some time, and even after the fall of the Roman Empire, there were attempts to bring back this position; and we know what happened to Napoleon Bonaparte who tried to do just that. During the Renaissance, Niccolò Machiavelli (1469-1527) came up with a manual called *Il Principe* in which he tried to teach his favored nobleman Giuliano de' Medici, the younger son of Lorenzo il Magnifico, how to acquire and maintain a principality. It most be mentioned that since Giuliano was the younger son, he was not going to inherit anything from the father due to the tradition that the firstborn inherited everything, so if he wanted to be a prince, he had to do so on his own. In view of the chaotic political situation in Italy during this time, it would have been easy for him to grab a piece of land and call it his own. Nothing happened because Giuliano died before he could take any action, and the only thing left, which gave the poor Machiavelli a bad name, was the well-known phrase, "the end justifies the means." Actually, if we take a closer look at his works, we can only see that he was trying to bring back some classic rules of the roman times: "Salus Publica Suprema Lex"(The good of the nation is the supreme law).

Better result was obtained by the *monarchy*. This type of government was very popular for centuries, and it still exists at the present time. While at the beginning it was absolute, which meant that the king could do as he pleased, later on, with the bad experience by Marie-Antoinette and Louis XVI with the guillotine during the French Revolution, a "constitutional" form of the monarchy was introduced. This meant that the people had the right to say something in what the government was doing. The king was surrounded by a bunch of courtesans who claimed to be a special class of people who called themselves nobles, and this position was obtained by birthrights. Along with the king, they did their best to enlarge the borders of the kingdom at the expense of the lives of their subjects, and in addition, they taxed them as much as possible so they could keep or expand their grandiose lifestyles. We still have the royal palaces, castles, summer residences, and all other memorabilia that prove how well they lived off the back of the population entrusted to their care. The sad part is that even now, there are some individuals that still believe to be a special breed with special rights that put them above the average people. Once more, if we look back and try to trace their origins, we can only find that at some point in the past, especially after the breakup of the Roman Empire, some soldiers of fortune, mercenaries, or other roughnecks decided to take over the control of as much land as they could grab and rule over it any way they wanted. Of course, they could not do so on their own so they surrounded themselves with other tough soldiers who later on received titles of nobility and control of some land, according to the amount of their help in creating the kingdom.

It is very surprising that even at the present time, in some other parts of the world, this practice is still going on; and some people, who consider themselves part of the nobility, really believe that they are a special breed of individuals designed by God to have special powers and privileges to be leaders of the rest of the people. And this "special gift" is transmitted from generation to generation. Fortunately, since it does not make any sense, this practice will soon disappear, thanks to a more advanced level of education of the people at large.

After the experience with the monarchies in recent years, we have experienced several cases of dictatorship with disastrous consequences for the people of the countries involved. Let's hope that better education, better understanding of the different cultures and religions, and higher living standards will make people understand that we are all equal and deserve the same opportunities to take advantage of what this earth has to offer, to live in peace, and to enjoy our lives.

Office of the president

We know that on this earth nothing is perfect, but some things are closer to perfection than others. At the present time, in the Western world, we have several democracies that based on some very fair constitutions, providing its people with a very good and efficient government. We can take as an example the government of the United States, which for the past century has provided its citizen with a fair and just government. Many people may disagree with this statement, but as mentioned before, nothing is perfect and there is always room for improvement. Many changes were, are, and will be made, but the most important thing is that the changes can be brought about in a peaceful way and are accepted at least by the majority of the people.

In spite of all the above, I can state without any doubt that any type of government could work perfectly, provided that the leaders and the citizens were honest, well educated, and full of wisdom. However, this is utopia, and it does not exist in our world, so we have to do the best with what we have. The government of the United States was very carefully set up with all sorts of checks and balances so that it would not be vulnerable to the possible abuses of dishonest leaders, willing to take advantage of their position to or enrich themselves at the expense of the rest of the people. We must agree that up to this point, it has worked quite well, and there is no reason to make any changes to its structure. But as I said before, there is nothing perfect, and there is always the opportunity to bring changes that could benefit the people of the nation. If we take into consideration, the main goals of a nation are (a) self-preservation, (b) welfare of its citizens, and (c) humanitarian issues. We can clearly see that we are way ahead of any other nations in achieving these goals, based on the level of our present standard of living.

Under the self-preservation policy, there are few things that could be improved. For example, why the whole nation panics when the president's life is threatened, and we take so many extremely sophisticated measures to prevent any possibility that this may happen. It looks like that out of the two hundreds millions of people living in this country, he is the only one that could make all the right decisions. At this point, we can see that for a single person he has too much power to make decisions that affects the well-being of the whole nation. We know that most decisions are made when a consensus is reached after lengthy deliberations with all the key officials in the executive branch of the government, but in some instances, he can act on his own initiative since he is the commander in chief of all armed forces. And being human, like any other person, there may be an instance when something would snap in his brains, and he may order some actions that could be very detrimental at present time to the whole nation, and to the whole world. It would not be a bad idea to modify his modus operandi and require that at least one more executive official, such as the vice president, or another assigned one also would approve all his decisions.

For the sake of national safety, it is also imperative that the draft for all the young people over eighteen must be reinstated. And it would apply also to females since they have emancipated to a point that they can do any job as well as boys. It is a familiar comment to hear military authorities complaining that the armed forces are short of personnel, and they have to adjust their military strategies according to the personnel available to them. This restriction can very well jeopardize the results of any military action with bad consequences for the welfare of the whole nation. Also, it is sad to see that only young boys have no means of going to college or engage in any other lucrative career end up joining the armed forces and in the time of crisis are the only ones who are available to fight for our country. Where is "justice for all"? The draft would also provide the nation with a tremendous amount of manpower available at anytime and even for any natural catastrophe, such as earthquakes, hurricanes, tidal waves, flooding, etc., that could occur in any part of the country. It would save lives and money, and it would bring back to normal the regions afflicted in a much shorter time. And even in normal circumstances, there is so much need of volunteers in hospitals, nursing homes, rehabilitation centers, homeless shelters, orphanages, etc., and many of the draftees, after the required basic training, could opt for a placement in any of these organizations according to their skills and preferences. Both the young draftees and society could benefit tremendously from this practice since the young people would be living on their own for the first time away from the family life they are used to and would be exposed to the different facets of life and learn how to deal with it. Society would benefit tremendously from the great amount of manpower available for free, would be able to give better service in all public centers, and this would compensate for the cost of the free education given to the children.

Another important issue concerning the welfare of the citizen is the right to carry guns, which is protected by the constitution and has been recently sanctioned and reaffirmed by the decision of the Supreme Court with the majority of five to four. Well at least not everybody thinks that it is a good practical law. We are all aware that the way of living has changed quite a bit from the time the constitution was written. There is no more "wild West" atmosphere, and even in the remote areas, people can buy food in the grocery stores; and there is no need to go hunting for it. Every community is quite well protected by the local and state police force, and there is no need for each citizen to carry these advanced automated weapons for their safety. It seems that most of the lawmakers stay away from the issue not because the change may be right or wrong, but it may make them unpopular with some of their constituents and could lose votes in the next election. The result is that firearms are all over the place, and any criminal or deranged individual can have access to them, including some emotionally young unstable people who have been able to massacre an enormous number of people for no reason at all. As far as the welfare of the citizen, we have come a long way in protecting the interest of the common people, but as I said before, there is always room for improvement at any level. There are always entrepreneurs trying to make easy dollars by promoting fraudulent products and services. In spite of controls, they manage to make money at the expense of credulous consumers who are always ready to accept deals and services that are too good to be true. A better control of the advertisement business must be exercised in order to ensure that the products and the services strictly conform to what is advertised and meet the necessary standards. Even the media should screen, the best way they can, what they advertise and should be held accountable for advertisements that are not truthful and that can be detrimental to the welfare of the common people. From the continuous scams that come up frequently, we can see that the agencies involved are not doing a proper job.

One of the most damaging practices that should be addressed for the welfare of the people is the right to strike. One of the best advances that the labor unions achieved in the past was the right to bargain a just compensation for the working people. It has worked very well in many situations, but in others, it has caused so much damage that in many cases, the employer was forced to go bankrupt because of the lack of profit in the exercise of the business involved. The employer lost his business and the employees lost their wages. So who won? As everything else in this world, everything has to have a fair balance, and the pendulum cannot swing more to one way than to another. Once the equilibrium is lost then everything collapses. But there are cases when this practice is not only unproductive and damaging, but also unfair to innocent bystanders. Such is the case when commuting or public services are involved. Millions of people are unable to get to work, millions of dollars in wages are lost, the lives of millions of people are negatively affected, and nobody gets anything positive out of the confusion. The fact is that after both parties bleed each other to death, in the end, an agreement is reached even if it is not the best solutions for all involved. In every negotiation, each party has to give up something in order to reach a solution. But if a solution is eventually found in all crises, why not reach it through a compulsory negotiation, under the supervision of a special commission made up by representatives of all parties involved plus other neutral authorities knowledgeable of labor relations and have the services go on as usual and avoid financial losses for all concerned?

It may sound a bit of a drastic and uncalled measure in a democracy, but the government should also be involved in controlling some of the astronomical salaries that are paid to people in sport, entertainment, and the administration of public corporations. It is true that we live in a free economy and that people can do and charge anything they want for their services, however, in many cases, all citizens are directly or indirectly paying for all of these salaries. For example, if we take a close look at the "obscene" salaries paid to some ball players to play a "game" that many other people do or used to do as pastime or for relaxation without any compensation, everybody must agree that it is unacceptable. In ancient civilizations, such as the Mayas in South America, death was the punishment for the members of the losing team, and even in that case, the financial compensation would be over the acceptable limits. It is true that some people get an extremely high satisfaction by watching the games and are willing the pay any amount of money to do so, but it is also true that some others would not pay two cents for it, but they are forced to pay for it indirectly since the advertisers recoup the great amount of money spent on TV spots during the games and other activities by raising the price of the goods that everyone has to buy. And the same can be said about singers, entertainers, and movie actors, and in the case of commercial corporations for whom a 20 or 40 percent profit should be the limit. Some form of cap or taxation must be devised so that the money extracted from the pockets of the common people can be returned to them to finance more vital services. And perhaps we should consider applying the same rules in the case of those immense fortunes that are passed on from one generation to generation. After a certain amount to the direct heirs, the rest should be inherited by all the people living in the nation, who most probably indirectly paid for, facilitated, and helped to create this wealth in the first place.

And before leaving this topic, we have to address another topic of interest for the government to control. We have laws that protect the humane treatment of all animals, and these laws are very actively applied as needed and for which we all should be very proud, but there is one instance when this law is not applied to humans. Maybe it is the source of a great amount of money to be made by many people, but nonetheless, it is a very barbaric, inhuman, and disgusting spectacle to see two human beings beating each other in a merciless manner, and sometimes causing irreparable damages to the individuals involved in this sport: boxing (in all its forms). It has been a very popular sport in the past, but it is time to eliminate it from our social activities if we want to call ourselves a civilized nation.

CHAPTER IX

Politics

In order to run a government of any type, a great number of people are needed for the many different jobs. Some are more important than others because they require that the people in some sensitive and high positions have to make very critical decisions that may affect a great number of people. In the United States, the great majority of the people working in the administrative fields obtain their jobs by passing the relative tests administered by the civil service, but people in charge of them usually are appointed to those positions or may be elected by the voters involved in their selection. While the requirements of the civil service tests may guarantee a minimum amount of "know how," and on the average, the citizen feel quite comfortable with it, even though there is a constant complaining about bureaucracy and bureaucrats, the quality of those people appointed or elected leaves us in the dark except for whatever information they want the public to know.

The most important decisions that are vital to the whole nation are made usually by a consensus reached among the executive, legislative, and judiciary branches of the government. The history books tell us of the shortcomings and the great things that our government accomplished in the past, and most of the time, they are pretty accurate with their evaluations. We have to accept the fact that our leaders did the best they could under the circumstances, but we could also speculate on the possibility that we could have done better if the caliber of our leaders had been superior. For example, would have been possible that if we had had leaders with better political skills, we could have obtained independence from England without the American War of Independence? And isn't there a possibility that the issues which led the United States to the bloody and destructive Civil War could have been resolved by peaceful negotiations? Some people may

The Capitol

say that it is only a wishful thinking, but past history indicates that people with great talents did and in some occasions accomplish political miracles.

After WWI, the United States tried to establish some safeguards in order to bring a permanent peace to the world, but it was a weak gesture. The policy adopted was to pay attention to the welfare of the Americans and let the European take care of their own problems. But later on, their problems became our own, and we had to go to war to correct the situation with a tremendous sacrifice of lives and resources that could have been used in a better way. Looking back at the whole scenario, it seems that if the United States had played a better role with regard to the political and economical situation in Europe, there could have been the possibility that those dictatorships would have not come to power, and the whole war could have been avoided, saving millions of lives and incalculable human resources that could have been used in a better way. Is that another wishful thinking? Maybe, but there are some valid truths in this point of view.

And so we finally brought peace to the world and immediately saw another dictator emerge from the ruin of the war: Stalin. Like an octopus, he managed to take possession of most of Europe and tried to take over the rest of the world. Could our leaders have prevented this terrible turn of events and have stopped him at that point? Who knows? The fact is that for half century, we had to face the cold war that brought us to the brink of a third world war, involved us in two unpopular and costly wars in Korea and Vietnam, which almost tore apart our society with antigovernment activities and civil chaos caused by them, not to mention the mishandling of the Cuban Revolution. By failing to support the Bay of Pigs Invasion as we had promised, we caused the loss of thousands of Cubans, and later on, we were facing the prospect of a nuclear war to remove the atomic bombs directed at our cities from Cuba. Whom shall we hold responsible for these terrible shortcomings? In a recent *Newsweek* article by F. Zakaria (July 7-14), "We Need a Wartime President," it read, "Perhaps the wisest American president during the cold war was Dwight Eisenhower, and his greatest virtues were those of balance, judgment and restraint. He knew we were in a contest with the Soviet Union, but—at a time when the rest of the country was vastly inflating the threat—he put it in considerable perspective. *Eisenhower refused to follow the French into Vietnam or support the British at Suez* [italics mine]. He turned down several requests for new weapons systems and missiles, and instead used defense dollars to build the interstate highway system and make other investments in improving America's economic competitiveness." Well, the accomplishments sound great, and at that time, this seemed to be the wisest decision from a domestic political point of view. But if we take in consideration that instead of helping the French retain control of that region, few years later, we had to go there and fight a disastrous war all by ourselves, and instead of supporting the British in regaining control of the Suez canal and establishing governments friendly to the West. For years we have been facing and fighting terrorist threats and continuous wars in that region, we most conclude that the policies adopted at that time were not in the best interest of our country and the world. Each one of us may reach his own conclusion, but the question still remains: could we have avoided some of those horrible disasters with better leadership in our government?

We are surrounded by a multitude of politicians, some of whom are great when dealing with the internal affairs of the nation, but they are not necessarily excellent in dealing with the foreign affairs of the country. One can be a great politician when it comes to domestic policies, but not necessarily a good statesman in dealing with foreign affairs, and this situation can be very detrimental to the very existence of a nation involved with so many problems all over the world. The way we select our president and members of the Congress leaves much to be desired. It is true that people vote for the candidate of their choice, but they have little to say in their selection. The parties select the candidates for a variety of reasons. It could be on the basis of their popularity, their appearance, their connections in the political arena, their ability to raise money for the party, their well-known family name, or their payback for favors received, and an infinity of other reasons. The candidate may have some great talents or may not, but once he is nominated, the whole pool of resources that the party can put together comes to his aid; and now the three-ring circus comes into action. Huge amounts of money are raised from individuals, institutions, commercial companies, and any other sources available. These funds are used to finance all sorts of opinion polls, TV ads, papers, road signs, and above all traveling expenses for the entourage that follows the candidate on his tours around the country. Speechwriters are busy preparing all sorts of speeches that promise everybody whatever they want to hear, and the candidates begin the verbal duel with the inevitable TV debates that are accurately scrutinized by the press, which announces the winner in the next few hours. And this goes on and on, and the press won't let it go until the election is over. While some people enjoy it, many others get sick and tired of the whole process and can't wait until the ordeal is over. Which candidate will win? Naturally, the one who has won most of the debates and has promised more improvements in the conditions of the country will win. But will he be able to deliver all that he has promised? Well, that is a different question. The future will tell. As things stand now, the public has no choice but to accept the existing practice that, hopefully in most cases, may bring about the election of a good average person. But we must admit that under this system, there is the possibility that a big charlatan could also be elected, and instead of improving things, he could create disastrous conditions for the country. Candidates should be selected on the basis of what they have accomplished, and not on what they promise to do as is the case in the selection of a Nobel Prize winner.

It is evident that the selection of our leaders is the most critical and important activity that we have to deal with for our own good and welfare. Yet the reality is that the majority of the people spends most of their free time completely immerse in the field of sport, music, and entertainment, and only once in a while they complain about the poor quality and the inefficiency of their political appointees. A great number of people know the names of all the players in their favorite sports team and for hours debate on the strategies that should be adopted to win the championship, but not too many of them know who is their congressman or senator that could make a great improvement in their living conditions. A long time ago, Voltaire said that people get "the kind of government that they deserve." And that is true because if everyone would take active part in the political process and put pressure on the legislators to enact the proper laws that could improve the quality of life at all levels, then no one would have reason to complain about the wasteful or ineffective policies adopted by the government at the local and national level.

Peace Palace, The Hague

The way we select our public official is not the best, and changes must be made to improve on it. Definitely, politics should not be another way to make a living because when people do that, they try their best to earn as much money as possible in providing the best living conditions for their family, raising their children, providing them with the best possible education, and setting some funds aside for the golden years. This could create a conflict of interest and lead some of them to unethical practices and behavior. For elected official in any key position, the age should be set at least in the sixties, and for the president at least sixty-five. At that time, they should be almost at the end of their careers and ready to enjoy retirement. Their need for wealth is diminished, their life accomplishments would be clearly visible, and all their knowledge would be turning into wisdom. At that time, they would be fully aware that their journey on this earth was coming to an end any time in the near future, and they would have to account for their actions to some higher authority. Only those people genuinely qualified and interested in the welfare of their country would volunteer their services. Their value as leaders would be determined by their accomplishments and not by promises of future utopia. There is no question that there are some young bright persons that could accomplish and perform greatly as elected officials, but that is an exception and not the rule. Age and life experience turns knowledge into wisdom and those are the qualifications that we should be looking for in the candidates for public positions.

In a recent TV program, they were talking about the present national budget in which there were twenty-eight billions of dollars hidden in earmarks. Out of the whole Congress, only sixteen representatives had abstained from doing so. If that money were to be spent judiciously, there would be no discussion, but in most cases, it was to be used for unnecessary projects or for some kind of subsidy to corporations, operating in the state the congressman was representing. Incidentally, some of these corporations were listed as contributors to the funds collected for the reelection of the congressman. Also lately, it seems that after retirement, legislators turn into lobbyists; and since they have personal friends still active in Congress, they have a great advantage in sponsoring legislation favorable to their sponsors. In addition, they can donate to any congressmen of their choice, the unspent money left in their reelection funds, which put a formidable weapon in their hands in order to have a favorable vote for the legislation they are sponsoring. If not illegal, this practice definitely is morally and ethically wrong since there are so many other very important programs that are desperately in need of funds. And we also have heard of generals who are in charge of purchasing goods and weapons for the armed forces. After retirement, they receive lucrative jobs as consultants or are given a seat on the board of directors of the company to whom they have awarded contracts while on active duty. And they go on spending billions of dollars in research and manufacturing of weapons so sophisticated and ahead of our times that cannot be used because there is no other hostile nation so advanced to require us to have these weapons. And the sad truth is that almost all of our soldiers are being killed by inexpensive homemade, roadside bombs, and we don't have a simple x-ray machine or some sort of laser gun that could detect them and save countless lives. This same machine could be used for the detections of drugs coming into this country hidden in the general merchandise. This system would make their detection a very simple routine, and with no drugs coming in the country, countless deaths and crimes would be prevented. There maybe be nothing illegal about the conduct of some of the high-ranking personnel, but for sure, the whole thing doesn't sound very practical or ethical.

LIFE: ITS PROBLEMS & SOME OF ITS UNANSWERABLE QUESTIONS

Sometimes with sadness, we realize that reelection and blind devotion to the party are the first priorities for some politicians at the expense of what could be the best policy for the welfare of the nation. For years, we have been discussing the terrible situation caused by the presence of about eleven millions of illegal immigrants. Everybody is complaining, but nobody is doing anything about it. The politicians are afraid of dealing with it because they may lose votes from the various ethnic groups and financial support from commercial and industrial companies that are reaping huge profits because of the low wages and no benefits paid to these people. Meanwhile, all social services that take care of them are on the verge of collapsing for the tremendous amount of money used for this purpose. And these funds that are raised through taxation and were intended for the welfare of the people of this country are creating more hardships for the overtaxed citizens of this country. Maybe I am a visionary, and I see things that others don't, but I think that this problem could be solved overnight by requiring employers to hire only documented legal residents or pay a stiff fine for each violation. Without a job, there would be no reason for anyone to stay in this country, and they would go home on their own without being deported saving us time and money.

The same can be said about certain practices that occur in the retirement of public personnel and officials. Since the pension is derived by the average salary received during the last three years of employment, many of them who have reached that stage are given all the possible available overtime so that their salaries for the last three years is way above the regular, and when the averages are determined their pensions are sometimes greater than their regular salaries. This practice could be very easily eliminated by passing the law stating that no one should receive a pension that is above 70 percent of their base salary. And then there is another unacceptable practice that grants congressmen an enormous amount of money in retirement pension even after serving only one term in office. Now, why they should be treated so generously while the average person has to sweat for this pension at least for twenty years or more, and also has to wait until sixty-five years of age before receiving a percentage of his salary as a pension? And naturally, we have the Supreme Court justices and other high-ranking officials that regardless of the time served can retire at sixty-five with their full salary. Why should they be treated so much better that the average citizen? Isn't this a clear demonstration that because of their position they can manage to pass laws that favor their own welfare regardless of ethical values?

At this point, we could take a look at another important issue that concerns the welfare of the people employed in any capacity at any level. In the past, the big business enterprises had a pretty well control of the politicians and laws governing labor and just about dictated the fair or better yet the unfair amount of compensation that each worker deserved. By looking at the documentaries on TV, it is very repulsive to see the conditions that human beings had to face just to stay alive. From slavery to shareholders, from jobs on the railroads to the ones in the coal mines and all other big construction projects on the railroads—the sacrifices of human lives was a negligible necessary evil, and the main purpose was to drain the last drop of blood from each worker involved. And they did, and they could because the market conditions were in their favor. When the alternative to low wages is starvation, there is not much of a choice. Finally, the labor unions came around and the shameful exploitation of the labor forces ended. But as soon as the unions acquired enough power, the pendulum swung the opposite way, and with the fierce competition from overseas, they caused many companies to go bankrupt. As everything in this world, equilibrium, or a fair balance, is the secret for existence and progress. So the question is what is a fair compensation for the different jobs that are available to the public?

In the past, the condition of the local economy dictated the amount that the workers could earn. Now with the free-world markets, the conditions are different since in some countries, conditions close to slave labor still exists; and it is impossible for the advanced societies to compete with it. Eventually these conditions will change, but meantime, we have to find a practical solution to the problem. The most advanced societies have to produce goods that require highly skilled labor not available to third world countries. So how we will arrive to a fair and just compensation? Well, each country has to determine at least the minimum salary that would provide a family with two children to live comfortably. It should cover the cost of the rent, food, transportation, medical attention, clothes, and other daily necessities needed for a decent standard of living. I mentioned the family with two children because due to the enormous increase in the world population, our means to provide for all the people are becoming scarce, and we have to reach a right balance in the world population so that civilization can go on and find acceptable solutions to this problem.

CHAPTER X

Justice

Justice

In order to keep control of the executive and the legislative branches of the government, the founding fathers created the Supreme Court of the United States. Its main purpose was to make sure that all laws and measures enacted by the other two branches were in accordance with the provisions of the constitution. Also, any case that could not be resolved at the local and state level would be review by this board of judges, appointed by the president with the approval of Congress. One would expect that they would be selected strictly on the basis of their accomplishment in their field. However, anytime there is a vacancy on this board, and a candidate is being considered; we invariably hear talks about the person leaning toward the left or the right, or being too liberal or too conservative. It gives the impression that *justice* is not one objective and universal principle, but whatever each person, on the base of his own convictions, wants it to be. So whatever is right and just for me not necessarily may be right and just for somebody else. It is a scary thought, but it is a possibility that could bring severe disagreements with unpleasant results even in an advanced and well-educated population. Again, there should be no room on this board for young members, no matter how bright they are. They may be hired as consultants or law clerks so that their talent may be put to good use, but all the decisions should be made by the mature, retired scholars who, after brilliant careers, decide to accept this position for the sole purpose of enhancing the applications of justice in our society.

Some of the cases they review should never have been brought to their attention since the decision on the matter in question affects people personally; and each individual should make a personal decision based on his religion, on his tradition, and should not be dictated by the law. In other cases, the matter should be presented directly to the public at large for a national referendum. What the founding fathers had in mind when they wrote the constitution and what the Supreme Court comes up with its decisions sometimes are worlds apart. The mere fact that not all decisions are unanimous shows that they do not come up with an absolute truth in resolving the issues presented to them. And to clarify these cases, we may mention again the debate on the *abortion*, which should be made by the individual according to his feelings and religious belief. And talking about religion and the state, we must take a look at some of the latest decisions made by the courts. We all agree to accept certain limitations imposed by the state for the well-being of all the people. But if these limits are carried too far, they may interfere with the "pursue of happiness" as guaranteed to us by the constitution. Our forefathers never intended to limit our religious expressions, and everything in government is saturated with religious quotations and symbols, such as "in God we trust," the ceremonial swearing on the Bible, and other traditional functions. The only reason they stressed the separation of the state from religion was to make sure that the government does not impose, endorse, or favor one religion over another. We don't need all that judicial expertise to have the proper interpretation of their intentions when they drafted the constitution. Still, lately, some unacceptable decisions have been made that negatively affects the rights of the people. The point in question is that since the state owns properties that belong to all citizens, the people should have the right to use them in any way they wish. So if some religious groups decide to decorate, perform ceremonies, or use some state properties or buildings to celebrate and fulfill their customs, they should be able to do so, provided all other religious groups are granted the same rights with the understanding that they are in good taste, legal, and that there are no threats to the public safety. We also should allow the teaching of any religion in the public schools, if there is a need or a request from the people in the community. Knowledge of other people's traditions and beliefs are always positive traits at anytime and in any place, and it can help improve the relations between people of different creeds and backgrounds by understanding each other better.

Another senseless and wasteful practice is the trial by jury. The law requires that anyone convicted of a crime should be tried by a jury of his peers. Many years ago, this practice was extremely important to protect people from being found guilty under undue and biased influences from flawed rules of faraway governments or rival political factions that were not acceptable to the local community. But things have changed for the better and now that practice is no longer necessary. There are proper laws that have been tested in all different courts of the nation, and the system has a very fair and proper way to apply them. It used to be that people were called for jury duty for a period of two weeks from eighth a.m. to four o'clock in the afternoon. Hundreds of people were milling around the county courthouse all day waiting to be called when juries had to be formed for a specific case. Now in some locations, the procedure has improved a little since one has only to call in by phone on the daily basis and has to go in only if needed. Still, this system is wasteful and does not fulfill its expected purpose. Groups of about twenty people are called at random, and they are taken into different rooms to be screened by the different district attorneys or lawyers appointed to the case. Both prosecutors and lawyers are looking for jurors who possibly could be sympathetic to their case and eliminate those that could be a liability to it. This procedure wastes a tremendous amount of time, and it is not foolproof because if someone wants to get on the jury, he can give any type of information or make comments that would favor his selection. On the other end, anyone who has other pressing things to do and does not want to be stuck sewing on a jury for a long and undetermined amount of time could say things that would disqualify him very easily.

If we take into consideration that the district attorneys obtain promotions on the bases of the number of cases won, and the defense lawyers become more popular and can charge higher fees according to the number of cases they win, then, without any attempt of being malicious, we can clearly reach the conclusion that the main objective of each one of them is limited to win the case and not to serve justice. There are many cases where the results reached are legal, but justice has not been served.

Also, in several cases of the same nature, different sentences are given for the same crime because the judges assigned to the case have different opinions. This is not an acceptable practice because the punishments involved many times go from one extreme to another, and it is not fair that one person should have a lighter sentence than another for the same crime. Like other judicial systems, a parameter should be established so that while the judge may have some leeway according to the fact emerging in the case, the resulting sentences should not be too far apart.

We also have to take a closer look at the time it takes for a jury to reach a verdict. In many cases, it takes too long, and all the courts in this country are so far behind that it takes years to resolve some very simple litigation. Again, we must take a look at other judicial systems around the world. Many of them use panels of other judges, lawyers, and legal experts. The prosecution presents its case, the defense theirs, and witnesses are heard, if there are any. On the base of the facts presented, it is very easy for the legal experts to reach a fair and just conclusion of the case.

As mentioned before, the main objective of anyone working for a living is to make as much money as possible by any legal means regardless of their ethical and moral value. This is why we have a tremendous amount of frivolous cases crowding the calendars of the courthouses, each one with the specific purpose of squeezing as much money as possible from corporation, insurance, and any other sources. The same can be said about all the other fields including doctors who perform all sorts of unnecessary tests and operations, politicians who are in it to grab as many benefits as possible, news people who misrepresent facts, mechanics who perform unnecessary repairs, etc.

Lately on TV, we see quite few ads from law firms expressing their concern for people who possibly have been hurt in accidents, by medications, malpractice, and any other causes. They sound so interested and worried about these people missing a chance to get whatever monetary compensation is due, and they invite them to contact their office where they could get a "free" consultation with an experienced lawyer and explore the possibilities of getting financial retributions for their suffering. It is so touching to see this noble gesture and concern for some unfortunate people, but knowing the fees that they charge after a settlement reached, it sounds more like sharks smelling blood and looking for a prey to feast on. The fee charged should be based on the amount of work done and not a percentage of the compensation obtained, which is awarded strictly for the welfare of the victim. Few years back, there was a case of a lawyer in Florida who won the case for that state against a tobacco company. The settlement required the company to pay back the billions of dollars spent by the state to take care of the people involved in this litigation, but the lawyer demanded that the percentage that he usually charged should be also applied in this case. It would have been hundreds and hundreds of millions of dollars, and frankly, nobody's labor is worth anywhere near that. The money is awarded for the victims, and not for the lawyers handling the case. All professional services should be evaluated, and fees set by a competent board for a just compensation.

One of the most deplorable situation occurs in the case of litigations due to malpractice in the field of medicine, accident, law enforcement, or other civil cases. It reminds us of a bunch of sharks in a feeding frenzy. The sky is the limit for the compensation of the pain and suffering. In many cases, we are facing an honest human mistake that nobody wanted to happen in the first place. Well, there is no question that the victim must receive all the necessary care and also financial means to be able to live a comfortable life according to his conditions, but the enormous amounts of money paid for the pain and suffering go way behind an acceptable limit, and society should consider eliminating it since it must be considered part of the possible negative experiences that invariably occur in the course of the human life. In addition, this money is paid indirectly by all members of the community with higher taxes and fees for services forced by the increase in the premiums paid for coverage by insurance policies. In the medical field, the guilty party should have the license to practice suspended and sent back to school to be retrained, and avoid the same mistake in the future. Also, by going back to practice, society would not lose the valuable skills and training of the person involved. In the field of law and order, demotion, suspension, retraining, and other practical and effective measures could be applied. The same procedures could be used in the settlement of all other cases.

Before leaving this topic, it must be mentioned that especially in the field of law enforcement, a higher level of education must be required. Even at the lowest level, a college degree is needed. Since a policeman comes in contact with all different kinds of people with different backgrounds and education, he should know how to handle each person properly. In all kinds of situations, there are different ways of dealing with the people involved. Also, this policy would prevent that some immature young man would go into this field for the simple reason of feeling important and seek and enjoy the feeling of authority that his position grants him. Good relations between the police and the citizen are a *must* for the well-being of any community. And in the case of minor infractions such as traffic violations, a *warning*, rather than a *violation* with relative fine would be more effective in keeping these relations at the highest level. The warning could be entered into the computer files and next time that this person is caught for the same offense, he would have less reason to argue about his innocence and should pay the fine applied for this violation without resentment. In many places, the traffic courts are so far behind that it takes months before a case comes up before a judge. This system may relieve the congestion in many of these places.

CHAPTER XI

Education

Ward Melville High School

The most important force that drives any community forward provides people with the highest living standards is quality *education*. A tremendous amount of money is being invested in it, but the results are not as good as expected. People mistakenly believe that the more money is spent, the better education is obtained. This is a very false assumption and very far from the truth. There is no question that money can make things much easier and improve to a certain degree the level of education of the people who want to learn, but it does not solve the problem of those who have no desire to improve themselves by obtaining an acceptable level of education.

In the past, and some of the older generation will remember, schools had no computers, no calculators, no overhead projectors, no movies, no laboratories, no cafeteria, no nurses, no buses, and other related programs to facilitate learning. There were only dedicated teachers with very low salaries, who did their best to explain in their own way the subject matter, and students performed according to their abilities and talents. The most important factor was the desire to learn, which was motivated by the pressure put on the students by their parents. The progress of the students in school was directly related to the social-economical level of their families. In many cases, education was the only way one could get away from the hardships of a low-income family life, and it was the only hope for a better future. Anyway, education went on; and those who wanted to develop their talents and had a strong desire to improve their lives achieved great results regardless of how the learning process took place. At the present times, there are some parents who, either do not care or are too busy with their own lives, dump their children on the school system and expect that it will take care of everything.

After WWII in the United States, there was a strong desire by all parents to give their kids a chance to improve their lives, and the state required that all children had to stay in school until they received their high school diplomas. However, things did not go according to the wishful expectations. Not all students were willing to work hard enough to fulfill their scholastic obligations, so the educational system was forced to water down the programs in order to keep the students in school until graduation. This also helped the administrators to show off statistics with fewer dropouts from the schools under their supervision and made them look good. This practice made the high school diploma lose its original value, and now the students, in order to have a complete and satisfactory education, have to go and graduate from college.

Many educators and politicians for the past fifty years have been trying to explain the failure of the schools in so many different ways. We still hear about "good schools" and "bad schools," "good teachers" and "bad teachers." Parents, when buying a home, look for it in the good school districts and most of the time force themselves to buy a house that they cannot afford, and sometimes after so many hardships, they end up being disappointed by the results. For several years, I worked in a district that had been recognized as a "school of excellence" by the state department, and most of the real estate agents in their advertisements would mention that the house for sale was located in the famous school district. Fifty percent of the students had above average grades and usually won trophies and admitted to prestigious universities and colleges. Most of them had parents who worked at the nearby university and hospital as professors and doctors, and for them, it came natural to follow their parents' foot steps; but for the rest of them who had blue-collar parents fell into the average and below average performance. So sometimes, we had to explain these parents why their kids did not receive high grades and give them reasons why the school had failed to educate them properly. Most of the time, the explanations were not satisfactory, and the teachers were accused of all sorts of negligent behavior—uncaring, poor teaching methods, and the most popular one, the personality and ethnic conflict between teacher and student.

As a child, I went to a school where all students came from the same ethnic group and had the same nationality and the same religion. The only differences among them were the social and economic levels. All teachers came from the same pool of applicants with the same qualifications and were appointed to their positions by a civil service system according to the vacancies available. Well, even under those conditions, the students' progress was always directly related to their family's social and economic levels. Without hesitation, I can state that the performance of the students has been, is, and will always be related to the value that the parents put on education and their personal involvement with the progress of their children. Of course, there will always be exceptions to the rule.

Then the question is, what is the best way to educate our children? Up to this point for some communities, the only practical method to give every child an education was to loosen up the requirements and allow all the students to go on the next grades regardless of their achievements, and we have seen cases were young people graduated from high school and were not able to read. Many people think that by throwing money at the problem, the situation would improve. That is not the case. It may slightly improve the situation but will not solve the real problem. Still, politicians and people at large blame the lack of money for the bad performance of the students especially in the poor socioeconomic areas. At this point, the cost of education in some places has reached such a prohibitive level that it has affected the living standards of the middle class in the United

States and has created so many hardships that many families have to move to other locations because they cannot afford to pay the school taxes in the towns where they live. And to make things even more unpalatable, it happens that some communities are blessed with some very high taxable real estate, such as power plants, industrial or commercial complexes; and they end up paying negligible amount of school taxes compared with some other districts. We can easily conclude that this system does not provide "justice for all" as mentioned in the pledge of allegiance.

So what is the solution to the two main problems? Exorbitant costs and poor education? First of all, better rules and more discipline must be implemented. For example, there are the cases in which for some personal reasons a student complains to his parents about a negative treatment or underserved grade received from a teacher. Since many of them have some guilty feelings for not spending enough time with their children, because of the job or other social obligations, to show their support and caring, in many instances, the parents do not evaluate the situation objectively and bring it to the attention of the principal demanding that something be done about it. Thinking about the possibility of facing and explaining his decision to the superintended, the principal is more inclined to please the parents. In the event the case goes up to that level, the superintendent does not want to be unpopular with the board of education who appointed him and pays him a very good salary for the work he does. Members of the board want to remain popular with the people who elected them and want to show that they have a good control of the school district and protect the rights of the parent and students; and in reaching a decision, they are influenced by the thought of the election coming up sooner or later. So, to whom does the teacher turn to for support? For him it is easer to apologize and heed to the recommendations or directions received from his superiors. After all, it is no secret that all parties involved have a paycheck to worry about, and in our times, there is no life without a paycheck. And principles and pride do not pay bills, And there is the student who, vindicated and being in the right, is bragging to all his friends about the incident, which will set the ground miles in case of other incidents between students and teachers.

To avoid being caught in unpleasant and unproductive situations, it is necessary to protect the whole educational system by creating a framework of rules and regulations that would not depend on individual decisions dictated by various pressure from different groups involved in it. My experience in the field of education made me come up with some possible changes that may help this process.

CHAPTER XII

Possible Solutions

The problem has to be addressed in two major fields, and first we look at it from the financial aspect. The following are some important steps to be considered:

Part I: On the Financial Aspect of the Problem

1. The role of the schools is no longer limited to educate the students in the different fields of study. Since in many cases, both parents work in order to be able to cover the cost of modern living, the school has to take over several tasks that parents did in the old days. In my days, my schedule in the secondary school consisted of five to six classes per day. We remained in the same classroom all the time, and only the teachers went from classroom to classroom. There was only one ten-minute break between the third and fourth periods. At that time we were allowed to go into the corridors, we could talk with friends, or we could remain in the classroom to review and prepare for the next class. If one had a snack, he could eat it at that time only. We walked to and from school regardless of the weather conditions and distances. Since no lockers were provided, we had to carry all our books and other necessities every day according to the scheduled activities. Nobody cared if you had had breakfast in the morning, and you ate lunch when you got back home. The students had to purchase all their books and school supplies. Discipline was very harsh. Either you behaved properly or you were out of school. No one went on to the next grade unless he passed all his subjects. In the case a student failed one or more subjects, he had to provide his own tutor, study during the summer, and go for a retest in the fall. If he passed the examinations, he

would go on to the next grade; otherwise, he would repeat the same grade. The teacher's decisions were never questioned or challenged. There were no school nurses and if a student became ill his parents were called and took him home.

Since then, the role of the school has changed quite a bit. We now provide transportation, books, cafeteria, health care, music programs, sports, after-school activities, counseling, tutoring, etc. Everybody agrees that all these educational aids provide a better environment for the educational process, then nobody should complain about the cost of education. And since it is evident that all these expenses cannot be provided at the local level, the only solution to this problem is to make the financial burden of education directly a responsibility of the state.

2. The educational system should be centralized at the state, or at least at the county level. At present, there is no reason to have a school district for every town or village. It creates a huge waste of human and financial resources. It is enough to think of the several hundreds of superintendents and their assistants with their big salaries. Millions of dollars could be saved by eliminating them since their job is mainly to go to conferences out of town, enjoying their big expense accounts, keep up with the latest educational news, attend the frequent board of education meetings, urge the educators to come up with some sensational good news about the progress of the students, reassure everyone that the kids in the district are doing a great job, and ask for more money to run the schools. Times have changed, and the local school boards in the old days were effective tools to ensure that the schools were training the students according to the needs of the community are no longer necessary. All members of the local board of education are there for many different reasons. Very few are genuinely interested in improving education, and even so, they would not know how. There may be some local business or professional persons trying to be in the limelight or to channel some contracts to their friends, several are real estate brokers who are interested in keeping the taxes low in the district in order to have a strong housing demand and higher sales, others may be simply driven by the desire to feel important by playing politics, and there may be some who want to be on the board simply because they have kids in school and want to be sure that their kids have preferential treatment by the school staff. At the present time, everything is so standardized that the social, commercial, and financial needs are the same all over the United States. No matter where you are, you see the same stores, the same cars, the same restaurants, gas stations, etc. The only difference from one city to another may be the weather conditions. With a centralized educational system, there would not be any more rich or poor school districts

because every school in the state would be provided with the same amount of educational tools and financial resources. At least we would not hear any more the excuse that the school was not able to meet the needs of the students because of the lack of funds.

3. We already know how much is the average cost of educating a student in the public school system. By adding up the number of students that would be attending school the following year, we would know exactly what would be the amount needed to finance the whole school system of the state. To be fair, the amount must be raised by a state income tax. This method would enlarge the tax base because each person with an income would be paying according to his earning capacity, and several working people may be living in the same house. Now, only the head of the household has to pay the school tax based on the fair market value of the house. The system is very unfair for the seniors who may not be working anymore and live on a fixed income, which has not increased for many years while the value of the houses in which they live has increased so much. In many cases, they are forced to move away from their homes because they cannot afford to pay the ever-rising school taxes. At this point, I would like to bring up the unbelievable amount of money earned by all those involved in professional sports. Some of the salaries earned by coaches and players and the team owners are by all standards inexcusable inflated, if not obscene for the work they perform. Why not give the franchise to the state colleges and universities so that the money earned could be used to take care of the educational needs rather than line up the packets of few individual at the expense of the community at large.

4. Schools would be built by the state according to the projected demographic needs. Now, we have the problem that while in one district a school is closed because there are not enough students, and in another they may have to build a new one because of the surge in the student population. And provided there are vacancies, students should be allowed to attend any school in the state as long as they provide their own transportation. This way, the complaint about segregated schools would go away.

5. The state would buy and distribute supplies to all schools according to their needs. This would eliminate a great number of related jobs at the local level and the possibility of local mismanagement and waste of funds as recent scandals in some districts have been brought to our attention. Every school would receive the same quantity and quality of tools and educational material, eliminating the label of rich and poor schools. Also, the greater buying power at the state level would guarantee much lower prices.

6. Many other jobs would be eliminated by having a central personnel office. Under this system, there would be only one panel for the negotiation of the contract, covering the salary for all teachers in the state. People have no idea of how much time and money is wasted in negotiating the contract for every village and town in the state. Also, the clerical and maintenance staff would be absorbed into the state civil service.

7. The state would directly appoint principals, assistant principals, and department chairmen according to established standards and qualifications. All superintendents and their assistants would be eliminated since there would be no need for them. This would create a great deal of savings, considering how high their salaries are. I am sure that the cost of education could be cut in one-half, therefore less money would have to be collected. Above all, it will guarantee that all children would receive the same kind of education, and nobody would blame the school for the poor performance of the students.

LIFE: ITS PROBLEMS & SOME OF ITS UNANSWERABLE QUESTIONS

Part II: On the Educational Aspect of the Problem

1. Since every school would have the same amount of financial funding, the label of poor school or rich school district would be eliminated. The State Education Central Office would directly provide every school with the same amount of educational tools and resources.

2. Teachers would be assigned to each school by a central personnel office from a pool of state's tested and approved candidates. No local board or principal would have any input on the selection of the staff. This procedure would eliminate the complaint that some districts are able to attract better teachers because they can afford to pay better salaries.

3. Principals, with the aid of the usual staff, would be in full control of the school to which they are assigned and would be accountable only to the Department of Education, and not to the local school boards. Among all the other qualifications, they should have at least twenty years of classroom experience (assistant principals, fifteen years and chairmen of the departments, ten years). This requirement would eliminate the possibility that some of these educators who did not have enough experience in the classroom and are not fully aware of all the problems and difficulties that teachers have to face in their daily routine would be in charge of their supervision. It is extremely important for the supervisors to have a well-rounded and extensive experience in the field of education since they are the only one who could help the newly appointed teachers to acquire the proper skills and improve their teaching methods. There are many cases where administrators are former teachers who did not feel comfortable or could not perform well in the classroom and had to move into administration to survive.

4. Teacher should be able to move from one school to another if there is a vacancy according to their seniority. Sometimes, the location of the school is not very comfortable because of the distance, traffic, or other family reasons. Other times, he may because a teacher may not feel very comfortable with the policies or the personality of its supervisor or whatever other reasons. A happy employee usually gives a better performance than an unhappy one. In the present system, teachers move up their salary scale, and it is very unlikely that they can be accepted in another district at their present salary levels. Unless there is a dire need for a teacher with special qualifications, districts prefer to hire teachers at an entry level. In a centralized system, this problem would not exist because all teachers would have the same contract and would keep their seniority regardless of the location or the school in which they

are assigned. One more important warning: there must not be no merit pay, because rather than teaching the proper way, teachers would be tempted to play the popularity game at the expense of a good educational practice.

5. It would be of great help if schools would require students to wear a uniform. This policy would eliminate all sorts of arguments about what is acceptable or not in a school environment. In the old days, people dressed up to be elegant, original, and in good taste. At present, the trend, especially among young people, is to be very daring and all in bad taste to attract as much attention as possible. Of course, the school should help pay the cost of the uniforms for the students who might prove to have a financial hardship. This requirement would create a better learning environment and make the students realize that the school is a special place that could influence the quality of their future and should be given the same respect as a house of worship. Most important in the secondary schools would be to have separate classes for boys and girls since children at this age are very much distracted by the attraction of the opposite sex, and they would concentrate better on their work if this situation did not exist.

6. Students must be allowed to learn according to their own abilities. They should not be rushed or pushed through the system and should go to the next grade only when they have mastered the required materials and skills. To make sure that this is accomplished, a state test should be administered at the end of each school year. The board of education should establish the minimum basic skills that would allow students to survive in our modern society and at the same time provided it with the skilled labor needed. After these skills are mastered in the lower grades, only then the students should be directed to pursue a field of learning for which they may have special attraction and talents. It is the responsibility of the school to make sure that each student discovers his own limitations and does not go chasing impossible dreams, and at the same time, he must be given the opportunity to discover his potential talents. One of the most important goals of the school is to make the young people become aware of special talents they may have in any field and be encouraged and directed to pursue learning in those fields. Our experience indicates that the majority of the workers reaches a certain level of expertise in their trade or profession, and they remain within that range for the rest of their lives. Very few excel to the extent of opening up new horizons with new discoveries in their fields. There is a possibility that with a better system, many more students could become aware of their special talents, and we could have many more people qualifying for the Nobel Prize. In order to accomplish this goal, it is strongly recommended that students

should be grouped in special classes according to their abilities. Having classes made up with students with different talents does not make any sense. It is like mixing good wine with cheap wine. We may end up with more wine, but all of inferior quality. The present system in many cases fails to challenge students to reach their potential, and they end up spending their lives doing average work and depriving society of a possible additional leap forward.

7. There should not be any real difficulties in applying new changes to the present educational system. The only real difficult problem is, and will be, how to deal with students who absolutely refuse to learn and create discipline problems in school, thus making the learning process more difficult for the other students. Some students respond to a strong counseling program; others don't. We must continue to work in order to find an acceptable solution. The best thing that we can do is to make them understand that if one has a good education, there is a better chance to succeed in life; otherwise, the losers will be forced to struggle through life to get only low-paying and undesirable jobs that are now being filled by illegal immigrants.

8. The learning experience mainly occurs in the classroom, and we have to make sure that this place is protected from all distracting and negative influences. Any student who cannot live up to the required rules should be removed at once, not only from the classroom but also from the entire school population. This way, he will not have an audience for which to perform and show off his macho attitude. All privileges must be suspended, and he should be kept in a special room during the entire school day and provided only with his school books. Incidentally, all school books should not be loaned to the students but rented to them. At the end of the school year, the rental fees would be returned to them, provided the books were kept in good conditions. At the present time, some students do not take good care of the books, and the district has to spend quite a bit of money replacing them.

9. If a student shows no desire to learn, he also should be removed before becoming a bad influence on the other students. It is true that the state has the obligations to educate all students, but this responsibility should end when the student shows no desire to learn. At that point, it is the responsibility of the parents to put their children on the right track. In many cases, some of them believe that their responsibility is limited to feeding and giving shelter to their kids meanwhile neglecting their daily supervision. It is only when they receive the report cards that they get shocked seeing the bad results and blamed the school for the poor performance of their kids. The close supervision in the education of their children should be part of their daily

life. This way, they would avoid unpleasant results and eliminate an additional burden on the community.

10. The schools could help this process by recognizing and rewarding the good students with all kinds of privileges and even financial rewards while taking all sorts of disciplinary actions and counseling programs for those who perform badly. It would not be a bad idea to keep the troublemakers longer in school, depriving them of the privilege to obtain a driving license at least until they are eighteen years old and going as far as imposing on them a special curfew after school.

Part III: Social and Civil Right Changes

It seems that anytime, parents, administrators or law enforcement officers want to take some action, they have to be very careful not to run into difficulties because of the protection and all the rights provided to the citizens by the constitution. This system is the best defense available to the people since history teaches us that authorities are very much inclined to abuse their powers and authority, but sometimes, if not very clearly stated, some provisions of it may create confusion and difficulties in its application. At this point, we have to clarify that there is a very big difference between human rights and civil rights. While all human beings, regardless of their race, nationality, and religion are protected from birth and throughout their lives by the human rights; civil rights on the other hand are obtained by the process of becoming citizen of a certain country, which provides them through the constitution adopted by the people. It is true that we become citizens at birth, but not all civil privileges are obtained at that time, and for some special activities, a person has to wait until he reaches the age of twenty-one before he can enjoy the full rights of the citizenship. For example, to drink alcoholic beverages, to join the military service, to vote, to sign legal papers, etc., there are age limits to be observed. There is a difference being a *minor* and an *adult* citizen. And this difference must be taken into consideration when dealing with children of school age. In the old days, there was a rule that accorded the school administrators the same authority of the parents (*in loco parentis*), but lately, even parents have lost a great deal of authority when dealing with their own kids.

At the present time, parents and administrators are very limited in their ability to supervise the kids because of certain legal complications. For example in school, authorities cannot have personal or locker search without due cause. They cannot have a random testing for drugs or cannot set standards for a dressing code, etc. Their decisions are always challenged from a legal standpoint, and in many cases, they maybe forced to look the other way to avoid being involved with all the unpleasant experiences of the legal process. It is obvious that these limitations help the kids abuse the system, which in turn, does not help very much the educational process. In this climate of confusion, it is possible that many parents do not know exactly how to act in case they decide to take some kind of disciplinary action to correct the behavior of their kids. And we cannot talk about *good parenting* or *bad parenting* because no matter what, in some cases, there are factors that are impossible to prevent; and even the best parents may find themselves facing a very sad and difficult situation. Sometime ago, there was an article about a single mother who was raising a teenage daughter. One night, the young girl did not come home by the time agreed, and the mother spent countless hours all through the night calling the police and all nearby hospitals, agonizing over the possible terrible things that could have happened. She had fallen asleep at a friend's house. Next morning when the daughter came home in the course of a heated argument, the mother lost control and slapped the girl. Next day the daughter reported this incident to the school authorities who in turn called the appropriate agency dealing with the protection of minors. They set up the girl in a private place, and the mother was forced to pay for all the expenses incurred until the situation was resolved. So much for parental authority!

It would be a great idea if the state would set up some kind of boarding schools, manned by a professional staff with fair and reasonable structure and rules and not too many frills. Naturally, it would have separate facilities or better yet different locations for boys and girls. This system would give parents who are notable to have a complete control of their children the possibility of giving the man an alternative choice. The young people would have the choice of accepting the parental standards of acceptable behavior or, if it was not reasonable to them, go to the boarding school. Naturally, the parents would have to pay for this service according to their financial capabilities, and the state would pickup the difference, especially in the case of low-income households. It may sound like an utopian dream, but with some sacrifices, it could be achieved; and the benefits for the parents, the children, and the community would be incalculable.

There is no question that children must be protected, loved, cared, and helped in every way possible, but when we get to the civil rights, we must expect that they have to earn those rights with age and education. They should wait to get those rights at least until they reach eighteen years of age, and in case they fail to graduate from high school, they should wait until the age of twenty-one, or until they join any branch of the military.

Since the state provides everyone with a free education, every young man and woman should give back something to the community upon graduation from high school and/or college. The best way to do so is to have them join the military or some other civil service units for at least eighteen months or preferably up to two years. This way, they would acquire additional skills, and the state would always have great available amount of manpower in case of war, natural disaster, such as hurricanes, tornados, earthquakes, flooding, etc. A tremendous amount of human resources would be readily available to bring humanitarian help to the affected areas without any financial hardship to the community affected. I heard recently on the news that they are having great difficulties to combat wildfires in California because there is not enough manpower available.

Also, with a certain amount of special training in their boot camp, these young people could be used to help in veterans' hospitals, rehabilitation centers, nursing home, civil defense, auxiliary local law enforcement, or whatever need may arise so that, in addition to the great financial benefits, the living standards of our society would improve greatly.

CHAPTER XIII

Additional Questions on Customs, Traditions, and Morality

We have seen that in order to live in a community, people have to give up some of their individual freedoms for the advantage of enjoying a better quality of life. First reason is safety because in unity, there is strength, and also because all the different and unique skills that each individual may have can be shared or used for the benefit of all other people in the community. In the early days, these rules were created by the need for a smooth and productive life of each individual, and everybody had no difficulty in accepting them. Later on when the communities became very large, some of these rules came from distant places and did not fulfill the needs and traditions of local people; therefore, there was always the desire to change them, sometimes by peaceful means and other times with violent actions.

Even at the present time, people have different living styles according to their geographical location, weather, and above all, according to the cultural level of their society. For example, people living in the tropical rain forest don't have the same need for clothes of those living in the far north regions of the earth. And between them, there is a vast span of different ways of dressing because of the different local weather conditions. The same can be said about food, shelter, traditions, cultural activities, etc. As long as people remain in their own territory, there is no problem because they live according to their established ways. It is when people cross their borders and come in contact with others with different traditions and cultures that some contrast come up, and most of the time, it is very difficult to avoid accepting one culture over another. One of the most practical examples of this situation would be the consumption of wine. For the majority of the southern European countries, wine is considered part of the family meal, and it is also used in the celebration of festive events. In many countries, there are no age limitations except that for the younger people. Some parents dilute it with water according to their ages. This practice could land many people in jail since it is against the law in all states. And even in this case, it would be best if the people involved would conform to the local laws rather than get involved in a lengthy legal confrontation. It is a no-win situation, even though the first miracle that Jesus accomplished was converting water into wine so the wedding celebrations could continue undisturbed. We don't know exactly how old he was when this miracle was performed. Since all people have different level of maturity, responsibility, and self-respect, not all the people should be treated the same way. Those who went over an acceptable limit should be punished and would learn from a practical point of view rather than forced to behave because of the law, and those with self-control would go on, enjoying undisturbed their traditions and celebrations.

In modern days, we have such large number of people migrating from one part of the world to another to a point that this problem has become very critical and threaten the stability of many nations. Fortunately, some of these living customs can be practiced privately, such as traditional celebrations, religions, foods, etc. and there is no reaction from the others; but when they become public and interact with other people's way of life, then there are some strong reactions by the public. Many rules and regulations are enacted in order to bring all these differences into acceptable practical form, but in many cases, they do not satisfy all the people involved. So in addition to the usual rules and regulations that need to be changed to improve living conditions in an established society, these differences create an additional problem. There may be several possible solutions, but it is difficult to know which ones will work best. Some of them may be covered by human rights and should not present any difficulty, but others may be of moral or ethical nature and need a more sensitive way to be dealt with.

In the case of the dressing code, many unwritten rules already exist since for many years the communities have established what is acceptable or not, and the same can be said about public behavior. Anyone going behind the acceptable standards may be prosecuted for "indecent exposure" or "disturbing the peace" and other infractions dictated by local ordinances. The community should always have the ultimate control of these rules and regulations. We have a recent case in a community in Florida where an ordinance was approved on the banning of low-crotch pants, showing the underwear. Those who don't agree have the choice of moving to another location friendlier to their standards. In the case of foreigners with different customs, it goes without saying that they have to accept the rules of the host country, or if not willing to do so, they should move somewhere else. For example, while it would be no problem if a person covered oneself from top to toes, for security reasons, it would be very dangerous to have people going around with their face covered. It must be understood that the rights guaranteed by the constitution, which was written only for the people of this country, should be used only for the protection of the rights of American citizens, and not just to anyone residing here. Already, the religious differences have been previously dealt with, and once more it should be stressed that for the better understanding of people with different religious beliefs, most of them should be taught in the public schools by professional teachers who could be more objective than the usual Sunday teachers.

Another topic that usually generates heated discussions and disagreements is the question of sex education in school. For some, the whole subject should be the prerogative of the parents, and not of the school; for others, the problem is at what age and how it should be taught since many children mature at different times. The solution is very simple. Those who want their children to receive this kind of education should be allowed to do so, and those who do not, should be free to have their choice. It is important that the schools have available for all students a counseling service to help them in case they have questions or special needs that they do not know how to deal with.

Now that we have opened this can of worms, we have to examine in depth all the different ramifications that this topic presents. Since the laws of each country are very different from one place to another, it is very difficult to determine what is the right and what is the wrong behavior in dealing with sex. The center of this discussion is mainly setting the age of consent for marriage and for sexual activity. Some countries don't have any age set and leave the decision on the parents if the persons involved are minors, and this practice may prove to be too liberal and not in the best interest of the minors involved. Some will be shocked to find out that in Yemen that age limit is as low as nine, and that in India, marriages are planned by the parents at any age for an actual future conclusion. Even in the United States, each state sets an age that goes from twelve to seventeen. What may be legal in one state is a crime in another state, and the individual involved may incur severe penalties. This proves to be a very difficult moral and legal issue since we believe that if something is wrong or right, it should be wrong or right anywhere all the time.

If we take a closer look at sex in general, in addition to one's personal opinions, we have to deal with traditional values, moral, legal and religious rules. There is no question that sex after food and sleep is one of the most vital needs that nature has put into human beings in order to ensure the continuity of the human race on this planet. Both in males and females, nature has created certain needs that can be satisfied only by the sexual activity that guarantees procreation. If we look into our past, we clearly see that sex has been one of the most powerful forces in any society, and for its sake, many crimes were and are committed. In modern times, it seems that our whole life is very much entangled in it. Every show, every product, every life event is somewhat connected with sex. It is only natural that many problems will derive from this state of being. Many religions have very strict rules and guidelines on sexual behavior and that provides answers for the majority of their followers, but for those who are not strong on religion and don't have any sense of direction, it is difficult to determine what is the right behavior when dealing with sex. In the past, the fear of pregnancy and the spread of diseases were a very powerful deterrent for abstaining sex. But know that these obstacles have been almost eliminated, people are left to their own decisions.

It is not easy to come up with universal rules on the sexual behavior, but some issues are easier than others. Everyone will agree that rape or sex obtained by any devious act is a terrible crime that must be punished to the full extent of the law. But even in these cases, we may come across situations which are on the borderline, and the possibility of punishing an innocent person is not in the best interest of justice. We are aware that men have a strong sex drive, and women have certain physical characteristics that stir and increase this sexual drive. This situation keeps some men in a constant activity to satisfy this urge and gives the woman the option and the means to intensify, encourage, or weaken the men's urge by her actions and especially by a dress and body language.

Many of these cases may take place in the so-called date rape. The bottom line is that both parties may have some responsibility on what and why it happened, and since many times there is no way to point out the guilty party, if a woman wants to hurt the man or get even for whatever reason, she may have an unfair advantage in doing so. As some girl put it, "We live in a society dominated by males. They in turn are controlled by their brains, which in turn are dominated by their penis, which are under the control of us, females." In some cases it may be fair to apply the same rules as in the case of an automobile accident where both drivers are found guilty to a certain percentage in causing the accident.

OBSERVATIONS II

Another very unfair application of the laws occurs in some cases of *statutory rape*. After puberty, some girls are so fully developed that it is very difficult to determine the right age, and for this mistake, a man can have his own life destroyed especially for the recent laws that requires that they be registered as sex offenders. With a criminal record of this nature, it becomes impossible for them to apply to any decent job, and their private lives are destroyed by the publication of their address with the public display of their photos labeling them sex predators. Recently, many TV programs have tried to bring this horrible situation to the attention of the public. The majority of these cases involves young people under the age of twenty. It is absolutely unacceptable for our society to see some young people who made the only mistake of falling in love at a very early age or under the pressure of a strong sexual drive that they haven't learned to control yet. To be put at the same level of hardened criminal and have their lives destroyed by something should not be considered a crime since most of the times it is consensual. They usually have caused no damage to anyone else or to themselves, but on the contrary, it brings some kind of fulfillment to them; and behind any doubt, it must not be considered a crime but at worst an unacceptable sexual behavior that can be corrected by a mandated strong personal counseling. It must be considered only an unfortunately family affair that should be dealt with by the parents of the children involved, according to their religious belief and accepted family standards. From an objective evaluation of this situation, it seems that the best age of consensus should be set for a legal standpoint at the time when a minor reaches puberty. Definitely, this age will not be accepted as normal by everyone. We have seen extremes on both sides of this issue. Recently, we had the case of a Middle East immigrant who killed his daughter because she was living according to the western way of life, and we have mothers who provide their daughters, as soon as puberty sets in with contraceptives to avoid pregnancy and diseases. If this policy does not seem to make any sense, then we should take a look at the recent statistics obtained through interviews with school children by a major TV network about this problem. It showed that 47 percent of the kids under seventeen have already experienced sex, and that number is on the increase. According to the existing laws, we will have almost 50 percent of our future population qualifying as criminals under the provision of sex predators. Of course, not everyone will be caught and prosecuted, but no matter what, these young kids will engage in sexual activity whether there is a law against it or not. Actually, most of them are too young to realize that they are breaking the law. This is another issue in which the state should have no business in attempting to control and leave the matter into the hands of the parents involved and let them decide on how to go about dealing with this issue according with their own values. And while on this topic, it is necessary to take a closer look at one of the oldest profession, commonly called prostitution. It has existed in the past, and in all very advanced societies, it was considered a very honorable profession. All the girls engaged in it were even kept in a temple of worship with all the rights and privileges accorded to priestess. With the advent of modern religions, this social activity was banned because it was considered sinful. But the practice was never eliminated and in spite of the laws against it, still it is very much alive and practiced all over the world, even in countries where a prostitute can be stoned to death. Evidently, it is a physical occurrence stronger than any human law, and it will exist in one form or another no matter what the governments do. Then the questions are: Why we waste so much time, energy, and resources in trying to eradicate this social activity that will not go away no matter what? Don't we have anything better to do with our law enforcement people? What is the nature of the crime committed and how it affects the people not involved with it?

There is absolutely no reason why two adult people cannot have sex if they so desire. As one call girl said in a TV show, "If other girls do it for nothing, why can't I do it for money?" And the truth is that many people use sex for an infinity of different reasons and not necessarily strictly for love. How many people marry for money, security, social position, and other convenient advantages that marriage can bring? In many cases, it is a barter tool, and while the format is different, the intent is the same. People have very vital and strong physical needs. When we are hungry, we go to a restaurant and eat, when we are thirsty we go to a bar and get something to drink, when we are tired we go to a hotel and sleep, and why if someone has a strong desire for sex should not have the possibility of going somewhere and take care of this urge in exchange for some money? This practice can provide a better protection against diseases and safety for the girls involved in this activity that now walk the streets unprotected and risking their lives because they come in contact with all kinds of criminals and insane people trying to take advantage of them. It would even create another considerable source of revenue for the state from the eventual taxes that would be imposed on this trade. And most important, we would be able to eliminate some of the sexual violence and crimes that takes place every day in our society because some individuals are not able to deal properly with their sexual needs and try to prey on some other innocent people causing incalculable physical and psychological damages that create a heavy burden on our communities.

CHAPTER XIV

Improvements on the Social Services

Advanced civilization

LIFE: IT'S PROBLEMS & SOME OF ITS UNANSWERABLE QUESTIONS

Everybody has to agree that the most important basic needs of the members of any society are food, shelter, and medical attention. Under the human rights, any state should be responsible to provide these basic necessities to anyone needing them at anytime throughout the life of each individual, regardless of the nationality of the person or the reason that caused it. During a lifetime, it is possible that any individual can find himself in dire need for some of these necessities, and it should be everyone's right to receive them without any question. What is the best way to apply this humanitarian assistance is a very difficult question, but we should be able to find a practical solution. At present, we have a welfare system that provides the indigents of all these needs as long as a person proves that he has no assets. Actually, the people in need prefer the services of charitable organizations to the ones provided by the public assistance, which are very limited and very deplorable quality in most of the cases. The medical attention is received through Medicaid at local clinics or at the emergency department of the local hospitals. Now, there may be a time in the life of a person who has some assets such as the house, a car, or other possessions when an unpredictable emergency arises, and this person has no money to pay for his immediate needs. In order to qualify for public assistance, he has to sell everything he owns, and only after he spends all his money he can receive these benefits. While he can obtain some relief for food and shelter from the private charities, provided he is able to swallow his pride, he has to pay for his medical services, and there is no question that all his assets will be sold to pay for them. Here we have double standards: some people have to pay for services that other people receive for free.

It is a fact that people, due to some unforeseen calamities or unfortunate incidents, may find themselves destitute at a certain time in their life. But it is also true that some of them did not live according to some practical standards or spend more that they made, or to a very extreme extent, refuse to work for a living, and society for humanitarian reasons takes care of them. On the other end, we may have someone who has worked very hard, made some great sacrifices to save as much as possible in order to have some assets that make life more comfortable, and this person has to give everything up to pay for the same services that others receive for free. It clearly shows that sometimes society rewards bad behavior and does not encourage good social practices.

It is a fact that all these free services are paid one way or another. The rich pay directly, and the state pays for the poor. The middle class pays indirectly through the insurance provided by the employer or directly if they don't have insurance. Some may have enough funds to cover these expenses, and others may face very difficult hardships that create resentment for the unjust way the society deals with the problem. To be fair and just, all these services should be given free to all citizens regardless of their financial status, and the state should raise the money through taxation, which guarantees that each person pays his share according to the earning capabilities. It is done in other countries, and in many cases, it works quite well.

One of the main objections to the system is the fear that the services will be very poor and there will be people ready to abuse it, making it too expensive to be practicable. Well, it is true that there is no perfect system as long as human beings are involved in it, but that is not a good reason for not trying. We can slowly make improvements to it, and in the long run, we may have an acceptable and satisfactory system. By requiring all health care providers such as medical doctors, dentists, and other related persons to work half of their time for a salary in public clinics and the rest of their time independently, we can give everybody a fair treatment. Anyone could use public facilities, and those who desired special attention and had the money to pay for it could use the private services. As far as the foreign residents who are a financial drain on our social services, the cost of their care should be billed to the governments of the countries they came from so they would be discouraged to come to this country to get free treatment.

Actually, a national credit card could be issued at birth to every citizen along with his social security number. At this point, it is necessary to point out that in order to receive the citizenship, one had to be born from a US citizen living this country. Anyone born to parents residing here illegally or just traveling here should not receive the citizenship automatically as it happens now. It would avoid all the unnecessary complications and discourage people to sneak into this country just for this purpose. During his lifetime, if a person needed some social services and was not able to pay for it, the amount could be charged against this card. The repayment would be due when this person was earning enough to do so or would be deducted from income tax returns from the proceeds of the sale of any real estate or upon his death from any assets left behind. This system would be a fair and equitable way to give the same treatment to all, and ensure that no one would get anything for free, and everybody would pay according to his means.

Anyone who has been in any branch of the military service remembers the boot training received during the first few months of the service. Recruits lived in one of the buildings on the base under the supervision of a person in charge of the unit. They were responsible to keep the place clean; they ate in the same cafeteria, which they manned in turn for the preparation of the food and the cleaning up after all meals were served. There was a chapel, a movie theater, a recreation hall, and also a small clinic to take care of their immediate emergencies. During the day, they went to different classes to learn some skills so they could

LIFE: ITS PROBLEMS & SOME OF ITS UNANSWERABLE QUESTIONS

become useful members and fulfill the needs of the service they had joined. It almost reminds us of a self-supporting gated community. Many of these bases are closed, abandoned, or waiting for some developer to turn them into shopping centers or housing developments since they don't bring in any revenue to the communities where they are located.

It is not unusual to hear that once in a while social service places entire families into motels or hotels at great expense to the taxpayers because housing is very difficult to find. These families have been evicted from their apartments or homes because they could not afford to pay the rent. In other cases, there are families with children that are forced to live in squalor, in very unsafe and filthy quarters in some slums of the cities. In all of these places—in addition to the physical unhealthy conditions—crime, vice, and drugs are rampant; and most of the children living under those conditions can only be expected to get involved in criminal activities and sooner or later end up in jail. This becomes a vicious cycle and also is a very heavy burden for any community in financial and human resources.

It may sound farfetched and idealistic, but it would not be such a bad idea to reactivate some of these empty bases and make them self-sufficient gated communities, where all the people assisted by the social services could be moved. The people living there could all take part in running its facilities. Under the supervision of some professional staff, all the people living there could be assigned to fill some special need of the community according to their skills and availability. Buses could take children to the regular schools, and some of the older persons could babysit for younger children while parents were in special classes learning skill which would provide them the necessary qualifications to get employment. Once fully employed and having enough financial resources, they would be able to rent a place in the regular community, move there, and live a normal life.

Under welfare, we can also take a look at the unbelievable number of fund-raising organizations operating around the country. When we deal with local people helping local churches raising some money, food, and toys during holidays to buy gifts for underprivileged children or food for families who are struggling to survive, there is no problem. It is a great show of good will and care on the part of the people engaged in it. But if a person is lucky enough to get his name on any mailing list, every month, a tremendous amount of fund-raising organizations send their reminder by mail soliciting contributions for their causes. It is true that one can ignore them, but by taking a closer look and see who are the beneficiaries of these charities, it can be very upsetting. The worst are those for the veterans in all different categories: paralyzed, wounded, mental disorders, unemployed, homeless, etc. These people went to war to defend our country, and now because of that, what have become of charity cases? Shouldn't we be ashamed of ourselves for these unacceptable conditions in which they are forced to live? The same can be said about the fund raising for widows and children of officers and other persons killed in the line of duty, trying to protect their fellow citizens. And the problem is even worst because it seems that nobody talks about it or does anything about it, especially the politicians.

More puzzling are the fund raising for research on the infinite health conditions that afflict society. One finds himself surrounded by a great number of solicitations for the different diseases. Sending something to each one of them will send you to the poor house. If anyone in the family is afflicted by a particular one, then the decision is easy, but if that is not the case, it is a very difficult choice. Any disease, if not taken care of, causes death. Should we make the choice based on the kind of death caused by the disease, or should we ignore it since when a person dies, it doesn't matter how it happened? Why should the individual citizen worry about the research for diseases that afflict the whole population of a nation in so many different ways? How can he decide which ones are more important than others? But the most important issue in all these fundraising is why some of the concerned citizens pay for it with their contributions? Because they feel responsible to do so according to their ethical principles while others who also benefit from these researches should ignore it and get the benefit for free? Since the health and the well-being of a nation is everybody's concern, every person should pay a fair share of it according to its means. It should be the state's responsibility to collect these funds through the regular income tax and directly establish and finance the cost of these special research centers in all state universities. But I guess raising taxes is a very risky business, and no politician will take a chance, become unpopular, and lose reelection.

As of now, the least they can do is to establish a special commission supervising the way the charitable funds are collected. As usual, as soon as sharks smell blood, they come in to feed on the potential victims, and the same occurs in this case. Some organizations specialize in raising funds for any purpose, however, they charge exorbitant fees. In some cases, it's up to 90 percent for "administrative" costs, and very little of the money collected goes to the charity involved. When a chairman of a charity was asked why they allowed this unfair practice, the answer was, "Well, suppose they raise one hundred thousand dollars, and they keep ninety thousands and give us ten thousands, don't you think that ten thousands is better than nothing?" Also, all the employees in charge of these organizations, except for those who are necessary to do labor work, should be volunteers since some of the salaries paid to some CEO are extremely high. It seems that they treat the organizations as "cash cows" rather than taking care of the people in distress.

CHAPTER XV

Dealing With Crime and Punishment

Law and order

Lately, the national statistics in the news claimed that over one million people are in jail in the United States at the present time, one for each one hundred adults; and this makes us the number one country with the greatest amount of people in jail. Either we have the greatest amount of criminal among us, or we are doing a better job in keeping them off the street. They also claim that the amount of violent crimes went down 25 percent. Good news and bad news, but the overall picture is not that good since the resources needed to deal with this enormous number of prisoners in our jails is a heavy burden on our nation. The majority of the crimes committed are drug related and committed by people involved in the traffic, sale, and use of drugs. Our government is using all resources necessary to eradicate this plague from our society. Almost every week we see that the law enforcement services confiscate tons and tons of all sorts of drugs, but its use is always on the rise, and we don't seem to get anywhere fighting it.

It looks like that whatever we are doing may help contain the spread of the disease, but it is not good enough to eliminate it. We have to seek the answer elsewhere and find different ways of dealing with the problem. The unquestionable truth is that if there were no users, there would not be any need for the production, traffic, and selling of the drugs—and the problem would disappear overnight. Are we doing anything about it? Sure we are, and countless millions of dollars are spent on rehabilitation centers, local clinics, counseling at all level, and the results are still negligible. Then it is evident that our methods are not very effective, and we need to study the problem and come up with a better way to solve it. First, we have to take a look at a person using drugs and find a better way in handling him. While in the case of minors, the parents have something to say, and they may use whatever tools are available to them in order to eliminate the addiction; on the adult level, there seems to be no way to force the individual to stop using drugs because the law says that he is supposed to be free to do whatever he wants according to his rights as long as he does not harm anyone. But the truth is that not only he is harming himself, but to procure money to buy drugs, he is forced to use any means, legal or illegal, to finance his habit. This is one of the reasons why our jail are so over crowded with people, committing nonviolent crimes to get their hands in any way they can on some money. And those caught are only the tip of the iceberg. Also, the temptation of making so much money in a very short time, and in an easy way, gets many other people in trouble by producing, transporting, and selling the drugs.

The overcrowding of the prisons, the lenient sentences, and early releases because of this social problem are another major reasons why people are tempted to try their luck in making a quick buck. And the vicious cycle goes on, and society suffers because of the destructive nature of this social disease. The only solution is to find a better way to deal with the situation. First step is to make sure that all people using drugs whether minors or adults are taken off the street. While this procedure would be easier with the minors because the cooperation of the parents would be taken for granted, with the adults, we would need some way to legalize it. Since they are not in control of their actions and the use of drugs makes them incapable of acting rationally, then they should be considered mentally disable and taken into protective custody. Also, one or more of their next of kin should have the authority to refer them to the proper authorities for possible confinement and treatment.

Since our treatments so far have given very negligible results, and many drug users after a short time go back to their old habit, our second step is to find a better way to cure them. The major excuse and a very true one is that they cannot resist the temptation of doing drugs. The actual physical and psychological need is much too strong to be ignored, and sooner or later, they fall for it. At this point, a scenario comes to my mind. Suppose they are brought to an island were no drugs are available, no matter how strong the need is, there is no way that they could satisfy their habit. It is true that they would have to go through a period of withdrawal, but after that, they would get used to live without drugs. So the question is: how can we build this artificial island around them? To accomplish this goal, it is necessary to put them in isolation for a certain amount of time, to be established by experienced and competent people, and according to the need of each individual. This treatment should cause a significant change in their personalities. And by isolation, I mean a strict one, with no magazines, TV, games, or reading materials of any type except some that would deal with their affliction. The idea is to make their time unpleasant and cheap because they would stay in their cells or rooms all day, and this would not require a large number of supervising personnel. This treatment would force them to have their minds reflect and concentrate on their unnecessary predicament and not wonder about other irrelevant topics. Food would be delivered to them in their rooms, very simple and just about enough to give them the necessary calories to be healthy. The diet and physical exercise would bring their bodies into the proper shape, especially in the case of their body being overweight and abused. At the present time, most of the treatments have a country club atmosphere and of such a limited time because of the prohibitive costs. As it is now, it can be considered a mini vacation, and going back to it does not have any deterrent for the patient. Again, the amount of time must be determined by the need of each patient and to be effective must be in terms of months and not days. It should not be considered a cruel punishment, but a necessary treatment since what we have now, in general, does not bring any good results. And if there is a relapse, the person involved would have to be confined for twice the duration of first time and so on, until he realizes that it does not pay to do drugs.

For all the other convicted criminals, the time spent in jail must be more effective and conducive to a better behavior after the release. The treatment they receive now is ridiculous and reminds me of the suggestions that Dr. Spock made sometime ago in bringing up our children. If everyone had followed his advice to the letter, the results would have been very unacceptable because the new generations would have not been able to cope of the stress of the daily life and would have had a very difficult time adjusting to it. The hardened criminals need a much more strict treatment than they receive under the present conditions. The expected rehabilitation does not take place under the present system and some criminals go in and out of jail without any concern. For some of them, jail time is a change from one social situation to another, if not better. They have three square meals a day, a clean place to sleep, quite a bit of recreation, medical and dental treatment if needed, counseling, and in some case, a chance for training or free education. As one single mother put it, "I can't take my daughter to the dentist because I don't have any money, and here, we have all these criminals in jail getting it for free!"

To begin with, any person convicted of a crime should immediately lose his civil rights and thus create fewer nuisances with all the legal demands and paperwork that sometimes inmates create. Everybody, same as for drug addicts, must go throughout a long period of isolation to reflect on their crimes and the reasons why they did it. It is absolutely necessary to erase or at least modify their existing tendencies or bad habits that make them lean toward an easy or violent way to make a living. The length of this isolation should be determined by the nature and gravity of the crime committed. The length of their isolation and detention will last until it has been determined behind any doubt that their wild and selfish personalities have been eliminated. At this new basic starting point and through proper counseling, they can be directed to learn positive skills necessary to live in our modern society. And at this time while still in confinement, all of them should start earning a living by working. There is no reason why the hard working citizen should be paying for their keep. Everybody works for a living and they should too. Those convicted of nonviolent crimes could be doing work for the community, and the violent ones would be working on jobs that could be done inside the jail. The earnings from their labor would reduce greatly the cost of their confinement, There should be no free lunch for anybody!

At this point, we can also take a look at the debate about the death penalty. Some are for it and others are against it since they claim that no human being has the authority to terminate the life of another. Some claim that life and death is only God's prerogative; in addition, it constitutes a severe and cruel punishment, which is against the provisions of the constitution. Frankly, the death penalty is a very expensive alternative because it takes many years of very intense legal work before the ultimate decision is made, and it is the easiest punishment for the criminal convicted of some heinous crime. It ends all his remorse and guilty feelings, if any, in few minutes. While by keeping him alive, he may be haunted for the rest of his life by the horrors and the recurring and repulsive visions of the crime committed.

CHAPTER XVI

Reality Check

Each person, by reading these observations, will find himself associated with one of the several social situations described. We are all under the influence of our own life experiences and may have different points of view on the many topics involved in the discussion. But regardless of our possible different opinions, we all have to agree that the human race has made tremendous advances and continue to advance in spite of the negative forces that seem to have a strong hold in about every civilized society. We have been through countless natural and social calamities, and regardless of the damages caused by them, human beings have been able to get back on their feet and continue the search for a better life. Where we get this resiliency and the strength to fight and stay on course is another crucial factor. It seems that the number one source of strength comes from religion, with the exception of those extreme forms of fanaticism which is self-defeating. The fear of God's punishment keeps most of the people on the right track and provides a strong backbone for all the people on earth. The strength and the depth of the faith changes from one person to another according to their life experiences, and we wonder why there are differences.

If we visit some of the places where the faithful claim that miracles have occurred, such as Lourdes, Fatima, Guadalupe, Mecca, etc., we are taken aback by the number of testimonies of miracles received by some of the believers and also by the behavior of those seeking a personal one. Some believe that these miracles cannot be explained from any scientific or rational point of view and are considered a direct intervention of God. Others are a little more skeptical and feel that may be the result of self-suggestion or some weird natural phenomena, and many more refuse to take time to look into their veracity or meditate about their meanings because they are much more interested in the next episode of their favored soap opera on TV or the results of the coming ball game of their beloved ball team. We have to accept each person's behavior, and hope that with a little more education, they may direct their energy toward a more important social activity. Personally, I had a strange experience; and frankly, I am still wondering what to make of it. And I am pretty sure that others cannot come up with a possible rational explanation.

Several years ago while reading a local New York paper, I came across a front page article, reporting an experience lived by one WWII pilot during the war activities. It was a common routine for the pilots of the bombers used in the air raids that when they were unable to unload their bombs on the primary target, they would have to look for a secondary target—or for safety reasons—get rid of them any place because it was dangerous to return to the base and land with a load of bombs on board. While this pilot was looking for a place to get rid of the bombs he was carrying aboard the plane, the face of a monk appeared in the sky in front of the plane and asked him not to unload any bombs in that region but to do so in the open sea, which was a safer solution for this particular crisis. Traumatized by this vision, he followed the suggestion; but he never mentioned his experience to anyone because he was afraid that nobody would believe his story and probably they would think that he was a mental case. The location of this experience was in the northern part of Puglia, which is a region of southern Italy. In that particular location, there is a monastery where for many years a monk called Padre Pio acquired the reputation of saint because of his miracles, and also because he had received the stigmata, which, for those people who don't know, are marks corresponding to those left on Christ's body by the crucifixion, and it is said to have appeared on the bodies of St. Francis of Assisi and others. We are not talking of tales related by third parties and for which we have no proof. The physical and spiritual conditions of this monk were analyzed and scrutinized very actively and closely his long life by the religious and medical authorities, and no one could come up with any explanation for the spiritual and physical condition of this monk. We are talking during the past fifty years when the latest equipments were available for all sorts of scientific and physical examinations. It so happened that one day, thirty or forty years after the incident, while reading a paper, this pilot came across an article about Padre Pio and a picture of the saint. Even after so many years while he never heard of him before, he immediately recognized him as the image of the monk who appeared in the sky in front of his windshield, and this time he did not hesitate in sharing and making public his incredible experience. I am trying to reach my own conclusion on this matter, and I wonder how anyone else will interpret this unusual and rare occurrence and evaluate it according to his spiritual background.

Whether we accept or not, these religious practices as part of the driving forces that sustain the move forward for all human beings, we have to admit that religion, in all its good forms, is a pillar that protects our civilization from extinction. Another strong support in that endeavor is the knowledge and wisdom acquired by those people who devote their lives in search of the absolute truth about the universe and the human presence on this planet. A very big threat to us comes from those people who only believe in their own selfish enhancement at the expense of other people regardless of any moral and ethical rules. Also, sometimes great harm and setbacks are caused by those who think they know more than they actually do and insist in forcing their misconceived decisions in the administration of the public policies of the nation. In this group, we have to list all those officials that one way or another manage to grab very important positions in the government of our national affairs without having the necessary skills to handle such important positions. The same must be said of those citizens who may be influenced and instigated by some wrong and shortsighted political points of view, come up with the wrong conclusions on some important decisions that are vital to the very preservation of our nation, and also interfere with the normal execution of the same by civil disobedience or other means. While they may think that they are doing a good thing for the country by exercising their right to disagree and steer the nation in the right direction with their short sights and ignorance of the facts, they may end up doing irreparable damage to the national security.

We can take for example the conclusion of the Korean War. The president, backed by the support of the politicians, decided to leave the country divided as it was before, even though so many hundreds of thousands of soldiers had lost their lives in that war to protect the freedom of millions of people. The alternative was to unite that country into one nation as suggested by the general in charge of the war. If we evaluate the decision made at that time against the situation at the present, we see that the country is still divided in two, and while the south under the democratic government has made such a great progress in the living, financial, and cultural fields, the northern part of the country, still under the communist regime, is starving to death and has become a threat to the world peace by selling or sharing their knowledge of the building and the delivery of the atom bombs to other rogue countries, which is a continuous threat to the peace of the free world. And nobody talks, puts any blame, or makes any comments on the validity of the decisions made fifty years ago.

Another clear example of the terrible consequences of unnecessary interference by private parties in the conduct of foreign affairs is the Vietnam War. Opposition to government policies is a healthy practice provided it is done properly. This was not the case in that war. It was stated by the Vietnamese authorities of the time that they were ready to seek peace and bring the war to an end as soon as the Americans reacted to their aggressive actions. But upon observing the open rebellion by so many American against the government policies, they decided to stick it out and have their enemy fight among themselves until they would get tired and quit. Well, this is exactly what happened. The cost: about fifty thousands US soldiers dead, millions of local people killed by the invading army, and millions more forced to live under the repressive rules of the communist regime, and the sad part is that all this unnecessary massacre of innocent people could have been avoided. I hope that all the responsible parties can sleep at night and not be kept awake by nightmares. And one of the most vociferous instigators of this rebellion against the government policies was a young little actress, whose name I don't want to glorify in this paper. It seems that some of these people in the entertainment business as soon as they get some success in their career and line their pockets with millions of dollars for work not worth a fraction of the amount paid for their services all of the sudden feel educated, intelligent, and superior to the rest of the people who pay the price to put them in that position. And even at the present time, we see people in that business probably with little or no education at all, making some incorrect, unsound, and dangerous statement on national foreign policies, using a podium not accessible to the other citizens. This is an unfair practice and should be stopped because it gives them an unfair and unearned privilege above the rest of the people. I am not denying them the right to express their opinion but that should be done privately and not publicly in a situation when they cannot be challenged by an opposite point of view.

Exactly the same problems are coming up now in connection with the present situation in the Middle East. There are those who believe that we are doing the right thing, those who feel that we are abusing our power as a strong nation and imposing our will on other people, and of course, those who could not care less about anything as long a paycheck comes every week, and they are able to go about their business undisturbed. Regardless of who is right and who is wrong, I am sure that we could have done much better in our struggle against the terrorists if our political decision makers and our generals in charge of the war had been of a superior caliber. And let me reiterated that there is always room for improvement at any level. The truth is that decisions were made by several responsible and knowledgeable people in the best interest of the nation. The fact that the results were not what everybody expected does not mean that we have to quit trying and turn our back to some important decisions that are vital to our survival. Sometimes, there are no easy ways to deal with difficult problems, and we have to struggle harder to solve them.

We already see people marching with signs, declaring that they want peace and to stop unnecessary killings of innocent people. How can anyone disagree with the demand for peace and unnecessary killings of human beings? But the true question is, peace at what price? Or the decision is, kill or get killed? Nobody comes up with the question: what is the alternative? Let us assume that we had not removed Saddam Hussein from power. Definitely, we would have enjoyed a period of relative peace, but for how long? We knew that he was ruthless and ready to eliminate anyone who happened to be in his way. From his actions, it was not difficult to see that he wanted to gain control of all the oil field in the Middle East and in doing so become able to put a choke on all the rest of the world by controlling its production and distribution. The only power that was able and willing to stop him was the United States. With all his illegal OA deals in the Oil-for-Food Programme, poorly controlled by the United Nations and condoned by other nations that were cashing in a considerable amount of dollars from this operation, he was amassing a tremendous amount of money that definitively would have given the possibility to buy or produce atomic weapons. At that point, he would feel very confident with his power of destruction that definitely would have confronted us directly or indirectly by using the terrorists. Would this situation be a better alternative? Would it be a better and fairer war if we had waited until he was in a better position to defend himself and cause us more damage and grief?

The sad part is that most of these conditions were created by the weak policies and incompetence of some of our past leaders. We relinquished the control of the Suez Canal, let some religious zealots take control and turn against us the people of some countries in the Middle East, ran away from Lebanon because of some heavy losses of marines, abandoned Somalia due to the poor results of our military intervention, and other related incidents. The results of our actions convinced our enemies that if they kicked our butt and created some painful experience for us, we would turn around and run. It was due to these miscalculations on their part based on our actions and reactions that now force us to face all these unpleasant problems. We often hear about the "imperialist America" trying to take control of the world, and nothing could be farther from the truth. We have done more than our share in bringing the world to the present conditions far superior to the older ones. Millions of Americans have died to liberate oppressed people all over the world. And after the war, we helped all the countries involved to get to their feet regardless of the role they played in the war. One has to look at Germany, France, Italy, and Japan to find out the extent of our involvement in helping them in the rebuilding of their countries. We never abandoned the Eastern European countries, we are trying to help the ones in the Far East and never refused to give a helping hand to any nation who asked for it. We are doing the best we can to

LIFE: ITS PROBLEMS & SOME OF ITS UNANSWERABLE QUESTIONS

help everyone and keep peace in the world, and still we are accused of all sorts of unethical practices and abuses on our part. It is about time to let the people of the world know who we are, where we come from, and where we want to go. We have nothing to hide, and we are proud of what we have done and are trying to accomplish. May God bless America!